A Pali-English G
of
Buddhist Technical Terms

Compiled by
Bhikkhu Ñāṇamoli

A Pali-English Glossary of Buddhist Technical Terms

Compiled by
Bhikkhu Ñāṇamoli

Edited by
Bhikkhu Bodhi

BUDDHIST PUBLICATION SOCIETY
KANDY SRI LANKA

First published in 1994
Second edition 2007

Buddhist Publication Society
P.O. Box 61
54, Sangharaja Mawatha
Kandy, Sri Lanka

National Library of Sri Lanka-
Cataloguing-in-Publication Data

Nanamoli, Bhikku
A Pali English Glossary of Buddhist Technical Terms/Bhikkhu Nanamoli - Kandy : Buddhist Publication Society Inc., 2007 - 161p ; 21 cm

ISBN 10 : 955-24-0086-4 Price : US$ 5.00
ISBN 13 : 978-955-24-0086-5

i. 294.303 DDC 21 ii. Title

1. Glossary 2. Buddhism

Typeset at the BPS
Text set in Palatino_BPS

Printed in Sri Lanka by
Ruchira Offset Printers
Kandy.

Contents

Editor's Preface *vi*
Introduction *xi*
Abbreviations & Notations *xv*

Part I: Pali-English Technical Glossary 1

Part II: Supplementary Glossaries 115

Grammatical Terms *117*
Plants & Flowers *127*
Months & Seasons *130*
Numbers & Measures *131*
Sanskrit Logical Terms *134*
About the Author *139*

Editor's Preface

During his eleven years in the Sangha, the English scholar-monk Bhikkhu Ñāṇamoli had translated into lucid English some of the most difficult and abstruse texts from the Pali Canon and its Commentaries. A distinguishing feature of his translation work was a sustained endeavour to develop a rigorously precise scheme of renderings for Buddhist technical terms. Though his scheme of translation underwent several stages of evolution, all these stages give evidence to an overriding concern with the accuracy and adequacy of the terminology he chose.

In several of his major publications—*The Path of Purification, Minor Readings and The Illustrator, The Guide*—Ven. Ñāṇamoli had appended a glossary of Pali technical terms appearing in the text, in which he also included words and word-meanings he had come across that were not in the Pali Text Society's *Pali-English Dictionary* (PED). In an appendix to *Minor Readings* he also explained his reasons for devising a new scheme of renderings to replace the one he had employed in earlier works, most notably in *The Path of Purification*. These glossaries attached to the specific works were combined and expanded upon in a more comprehensive glossary that Ven. Ñāṇamoli had compiled, apparently for his own use and to share with a few fellow-scholars of the Pali texts. To my knowledge only three copies of this glossary were prepared by Ven. Ñāṇamoli himself. One now belongs to the library of the Island Hermitage at Dodanduwa, where he had spent his entire life as a monk. A second was sent to Ven. Nyanaponika Mahāthera and has been kept all these years at the Forest Hermitage in Kandy. The third had belonged to I.B. Horner, late president of the Pali Text Society, and is now in the possession of K.R. Norman, the Society's current president.

The copies at the Island Hermitage and the Forest Hermitage are both carbons consisting of about 120 typed pages. The Forest Hermitage copy is dated 1956 and also contains, as a tucked-in enclosure, a set of additions and corrections dated 1957. The Island Hermitage copy has the same enclosure but without dates. The pages of the original glossary are themselves strewn with additions and corrections, some typed in, others entered in pencil in Ven. Ñāṇamoli's own handwriting. It is quite likely that he continued to make minor changes in the glossary and to fill in references right up to his death in 1960.

In his introductory note Ven. Ñāṇamoli had remarked that the glossary is both incomplete and provisional. Almost certainly he had no intention of publishing it but had compiled it primarily to guide his own translations. Nevertheless, those few of us who have had access to the typed glossary have found it very helpful in our studies. It is with the thought that this glossary could be of use to a wider circle of scholars and students that the Buddhist Publication Society is issuing it in this printed edition.

My own hand in editing the material in the technical glossary has been very light. I wished to keep the glossary in its entirety the work of Ven. Ñāṇamoli and not treat his collection of terms as the starting point for a larger technical dictionary. In preparing the work for publication I compared the two copies available to me—the Island Hermitage copy and the Forest Hermitage copy—and where I found minor discrepancies between them (there were very few) I chose the reading that seemed more satisfactory. I have, of course, incorporated the list of additions and corrections directly into the body of the glossary. I also scanned the glossaries at the back of his published works and found a number of technical terms not included in the original glossary; these have now been incorporated. Several terms have also been gleaned from his marginal notes to his personal copy of the P.T.S. dictionary and from his manuscript notes to his translation of the Majjhima Nikāya. I staunchly resisted the temptation to add new entries on my own, though an exception was made for the compound *karaṇa-sādhana*. This is the third member of a traditional triad of which Ven.

Ñāṇamoli had included the other two members but for some reason had omitted this third member.

Since he had prepared the glossary principally for his private use, Ven. Ñāṇamoli had attempted to restrict his choice of renderings to those he would employ in the translation work with which he was occupied concurrently with the compilation of the glossary. In some instances, when I thought the reader needed more help to grasp the meaning of a term, I have added other renderings, including those used by Ven. Ñāṇamoli in his previous translation scheme. In all cases, with one exception, these additions have been enclosed in angle brackets (< >). The exception is the rendering of *citta*. Ven. Ñāṇamoli had chosen to render this common Pali word as "cognizance," and had used this rendering consistently in the glossary as well as in his later translations. Although I left "cognizance" as the primary rendering under *citta*, in the numerous compounds that include *citta* I have replaced "cognizance" by the more familiar "consciousness," or in some instances, by "mind." These were the renderings Ven. Ñāṇamoli had used in his earlier scheme, and it seems he adopted "cognizance" for *citta* only because he wanted to maintain, in translation, the distinctions between the Pali words *citta*, *mano*, and *viññāṇa*.

Sometimes Ven. Ñāṇamoli had included in the glossary Pali terms for which he had not provided a meaning. When I could find or determine the meaning I have added it, again in angle brackets, but when this was not possible the term had to be left undefined. Unfortunately, in a fair number of references Ven. Ñāṇamoli had given merely the source work but not a page number. This was especially common with his references to the *Aṅguttara Aṭṭhakathā* and the *Visuddhimagga Aṭṭhakathā*. Constraints of time made it impossible for me to trace these references and they therefore had to be left incomplete. Again, owing to constraints of time, I could not double-check all of Ven. Ñāṇamoli's references, and thus many have been accepted on trust as correct. A fellow monk, however, did double-check numerous references to the commentaries, which in a few cases had to be corrected. I also managed to track down Ven. Ñāṇamoli's references to the Itivuttaka Aṭṭhakathā and the Udāna Aṭṭhakathā, for which he employed Sinhala-script editions, and have replaced the page numbers with those of the P.T.S. editions.

The use of square brackets ([ ]) and braces ({ }) to represent, respectively, the sources giving formal definitions of terms and enumerations of kinds, has been introduced in this edition. The typescript employed only parentheses for all supplementary matter.

Besides his main technical glossary, Ven. Ñāṇamoli had also compiled, in a separate notebook, what he called an "appendix to the P.T.S 's Pali-English Dictionary" and supplementary lists of specialized Pali terms. These were all written in ink (except a few provisional entries that were in pencil), with ample space between entries to accommodate additions which he must have expected to encounter in his readings. Virtually all the items in the "appendix" were already included in the technical glossary as the terms marked by an asterisk. However, for the sake of completeness I thought it would be of benefit to include here, as supplementary glossaries, the lists of specialized terms. Even though some of these terms already appear in the main glossary in their proper alphabetical position, their inclusion again by way of topic should facilitate access to them.

These supplementary glossaries make even less of a claim to completeness and adequacy than the main glossary. It is evident that Ven. Ñāṇamoli had not made any systematic attempt to collect all the important terms under the topics heading the lists, but had merely recorded the sets of terms he came across in his reading. For example, the list of plants and flowers draws upon only a very few works and could have been greatly extended if the Vinaya Piṭaka and the Jātakas had been consulted. Some of his schemata under the heading of "numbers and measures" seem hypothetical, and his notebook here is dotted with question marks. The list of Sanskrit logical terms refers to a single source (*Primer of Indian Logic* by S. Kuppuswami Sastri) and may have been based entirely on that work.

In editing the supplementary glossaries I have felt less bound to the original manuscript than in editing the main glossary. The list of grammatical terms has, to some extent, been reorganized and expanded by a few additions of important grammatical terms taken from A.K. Warder's *Introduction to Pali* (P.T.S. 1963) and Ven. A.P. Buddhadatta's *New Pali Course*, Part 2 (Colombo 1956). The latter work seems to be the source from which Ven. Ñāṇamoli had extracted his examples of the different kinds of compounds. The lists of numbers and measures were also partly reorganized, but while I double-checked those schemata for which Ven. Ñāṇamoli provided a textual source, I could not double-check those for which a source was not indicated.

BHIKKHU BODHI

Note to Second Edition

A number of minor changes and corrections, mostly dealing with style, have been made to this edition. The abbreviations of Pali texts have been brought in line with the internationally accepted abbreviation scheme given in the *Critical Pali Dictionary*.

BHIKKHU ÑĀṆATUSITA

Introduction

1. *Scope*: This glossary is restricted to: (a) epistemological, psychological, philosophical, etc., words and meanings of a technical or semi-technical nature (Vinaya excluded); (b) "enumerations"; and (c) words and meanings not in the PED (marked with an asterisk *).

2. It is both *incomplete,* because few books have been collated, and it is also *provisional,* because there is more to be done in the matter of clearing up meanings.

3. *Aims*: Under 1 (a) to try to produce a practical set of English equivalents for Pali technical terms: one that can be made to work, rendering the sense with due regard to contexts and connected passages, and also to English usage. The present situation with its multiplication of variants for one idea, its poverty of terms for many ideas, and its many serious inaccuracies, tends to chaos. The scheme put forward is not claimed as the only one; a partial alternative is given below, but alterations should be made with due regard to the general allotment of terms.

4. *Renderings* have been chosen with an eye on consistent handling of roots (as far as possible), on compatibility with varying contexts and actual ideas symbolized, and on usage (e.g. the derivations of *bhū* that carry definite ontological connection with the *bhava* of the *paṭicca-samuppāda* formulation in its various contexts). There is no space here to consider the *allotment of terms*.

5. *Enumerations* (e.g. "4 *satipaṭṭhāna,*" "108 *vedanā,*" etc.) are usually not given if already in the PED; otherwise they are given with a reference. The numerical series in the Aṅguttara Nikāya, Itivuttaka, and the last two suttas of the Dīgha Nikāya should also be consulted.

6. *Definitions*: some references for principal definitions of important terms are given.

7. *Words not in PED* are from few sources. The Visuddhimagga, Majjhima Nikāya, Paṭisambhidāmagga and Sammohavinodanī have been combed, M-a and Vism-a partially, and others mentioned sporadically treated. Some meanings need verifying.

8. If "idea" is not liked for *dhamma*, the only alternatives are to leave it untranslated or to revert to fragmentation (even as it is, one or two idiomatic phrases remain refractory). "Idea" for *dhamma* does *not* imply "the world is nothing but ideas," which the use of the word in its contexts should make clear.

9. The frequent important plays on the words *brahma* and *brāhmaṇa* can be handled if the following scheme is adopted, which has much to support it both etymologically and semantically: *brahma* = divine; *Brahmā* = (the) Divine; *brāhmaṇa* = (priestly) divine.

BHIKKHU ÑĀṆAMOLI

Alternative Scheme of Renderings For Certain Principal Words

Pali	Rendering Adopted	Alternative
rūpa	form	matter, materiality
rūpa-kkhandha	form aggregate	materiality aggregate
rūpāyatana	form base	visible-object base
arūpa	formless	immaterial
āruppa	formless state	immaterial state
nāma-rūpa	name-and-form	mentality-materiality
nāma	name	mentality name
dabba	matter	material
saṅkharoti *abhisaṅkharoti*	to determine	to form
saṅkhāra *abhisaṅkhāra*	determination	formation
saṅkhata *abhisaṅkhata*	determined	formed
asaṅkhata	undetermined	unformed
avyākata	undeclared	indeterminate
dhamma	idea, True Idea, ideal, etc.	dhamma, Dhamma, law, state, etc.

Roots Of Special Importance Requiring Particular Attention

ROOT	MEANING
bhū (hu)	being, to be becoming to become
as	there is essence state entity

ROOT		MEANING
pad		to appear to have a manner to practice a way
vid	*ved*	(a) to feel
	vind	(b) to know
dhar		to hear, remember
jā		to know

Principle Words for "Mind" and "Consciousness"

ROOT	WORD	TECHNICAL USAGE	LOOSE USAGE
cit (to vary, to think)	*cetanā*	= *kamma*	intention
	ceto	e.g., *cetovimutti*	mind, heart
	citta	e.g., *akusala-citta*	to know
man (to measure)	*mano*	*manāyatana* *mano-viññāṇa*	synonyms for mind and conscious-ness
jā (to know)	*viññāṇa*	e.g., *cakkhu-viññāṇa* e.g., *viññāṇa-kkhanda*	

Abbreviations & Notations

ABBREVIATIONS OF TEXTS

References are to P.T.S. editions unless otherwise stated

A	Aṅguttara Nikāya
A-a	*Aṅguttara Nikāya Aṭṭhakathā/Manorathapūraṇī*
Abh	*Abhidhānappadīpikā*
Abhi-av	*Abhidhammāvatāra*
Abhidh-s	*Abhidhammatthasaṅgaha*
As	*Atthasālinī /Dhammasaṅganī Aṭṭhakathā*
As-mṭ	*Dhammasaṅgaṇī Mūla-ṭikā* Pt. I (Be)
It	Itivuttaka
It-a	*Itivuttaka Aṭṭhakathā*
Ud	Udāna
Ud-a	*Udāna Aṭṭhakathā*
Ja	*Jātaka Aṭṭhakathā*
Kkh	*Kaṅkhāvitaraṅī/Pāṭimokkha Aṭṭhakathā*
Kv	Kathāvatthu
Khuddas	*Khuddasikkhā* (verse no.)
Khuddas-nṭ	*Khuddasikkhā Aṭṭhakathā/Sumaṅgalapasādanī*
Khp	Khuddakapāṭha
Th-a	*Theragāthā Aṭṭhakathā*
D	Dīgha Nikāya (DN = Dīgha Nikāya Sutta)
D-a	*Dīgha Nikāya Aṭṭhakathā/Sumaṅgalavilāsinī*
Dhp	Dhammapada
Dhs	*Dhammasaṅgaṇī* (§ no.)
Nidd I	Mahāniddesa
Nidd II	Cūḷaniddesa
Nett	Nettippakaraṇa
Paṭṭh	Paṭṭhāna
Paṭis	Paṭisambhidāmagga

Paṭis-a	*Paṭisambhidāmagga Aṭṭhakathā/ Saddhammappakāsinī*
Pp-a	*Puggalapaññatti Aṭṭhakathā*
Pv	Petavatthu
M	Majjhima Nikāya (MN = Majjhima Nikāya Sutta)
M-a	*Majjhima Nikāya Aṭṭhakathā/Papañcasūdanī*
Mil	*Milindapañha*
M-ṭ	*Majjhima Nikāya Ṭīkā* (Be)
Mv	*Mahāvaṃsa* (ch. & v.)
Yam	Yamaka
Vin I	Vinaya Mahāvagga
Vin II	Vinaya Cūḷavagga
Vin III	Vinaya Suttavibhaṅga I
Vin IV	Vinaya Suttavibhaṅga II
Vin-a	*Vinaya Aṭṭhakathā/Samantapāsādikā*
Vin-vn	*Vinaya-vinicchaya*
Vibh	Vibhaṅga
Vibh-a	*Vibhaṅga Aṭṭhakathā/Sammohavinodanī*
Vibh-mṭ	*Vibhaṅga Mūla-ṭīkā* Pt. II (Be)
Vism	*Visuddhimagga*
Vism-a	*Visuddhimagga Aṭṭhakathā/Mahā-ṭīkā/ Paramatthamañjūsā***
S	Saṃyutta Nikāya
S-a	*Saṃyutta Nikāya Aṭṭhakathā/Sāratthappakāsinī*
Sp-ṭ	*Sāratthadīpanī Vinaya Ṭīkā* (Be)
Sn	Suttanipāta
Sn-a	*Suttanipāta Aṭṭhakathā*

* Chs. i-xvii Ce; Chs. xviii-xxiii Be. Refs. up to p. 645 are to Ce; refs. from p. 744 and higher are to Be.

ABBREVIATIONS OF WORDS

absol.	absolutive
abstr.	abstract
adj.	adjective
adv.	adverb
aor.	aorist
Be.	Burmese ed. (CS)
caus.	causative
Ce.	Ceylon ed. (Sri Lanka)
cf.	compare
comy.	commentary
cons.	consonant
CPD	Critical Pali Dictionary
decl.	declinable
def.	definition
ed.	edition
Ee.	European ed. (P.T.S.)
encl.	enclitic
f.	and forward
ff.	and forward (plural)
fem.	feminine
fr.	from
gen.	genitive
ger.	gerund
gram.	grammar
imp.	imperative
inf.	infinitive
kds.	kinds
log.	logic
masc.	masculine
n.	noun
no.	number
opp.	opposite
p.	page
pass.	passive

pers.	person
PED	Pali English Dictionary (P.T.S.)
prep.	preposition
ppr.	present participle
pl.	plural
pp.	past participle
P.T.S.	Pali Text Society
q.v.	which see
sing.	singular
v.	verse

NOTATIONS

*	word, or that meaning of the word, is not in the PED
[ ]	source for the definition of a term
{ }	source for the enumeration of a term
< >	enclosed text added by editor

PART I:

PALI-ENGLISH TECHNICAL GLOSSARY

A

***aṃsa**—a disease (piles? *Catubhānavāra* suggests phymosis): A V 110

akiñcana—non-impediment, non-owning; <nothing>

akiriya-diṭṭhi, akiriya-vāda—view or theory that there is no ripening of action (= *akamma-vāda*)

akuppa—unassailable, <unshakable>

akusala—(1) unskilful; (2) (kammically) unprofitable, <unwholesome> {3 kinds: *see*: *mūla*, *vitakka*, *saṅkappa*, and *saññā*}

akkosavatthu—example of abuse {the 10: Vibh-a 340; S-a I 342}

agati—(1) bad destination {the 4: Vism 683}; (2) no destination (= *nibbāna*: Vibh-a 400) [def. Vism 683]

***agaru**—aloe wood: Vism 241 (see *agaḷu* in PED)

agocara—wrong resort {the 5: Vibh 247; 6 kinds: M-a III 5}

aṅga—(1) limb; (2) factor, member (of path, jhāna, etc.); *see dhutaṅga*

***aṅgirasa**—of radiant limbs (epithet of the Buddha): A III 239

aṅguli—(1) finger, toe; (2) measure of length (7 *dhaññamāsa* = 1 a.; 12 a. = 1 *vidatthi*)

acala-cetiya-ṭṭhāna—permanent shrine site {the 4: M-a II 166}

acinteyya, acintaya—unthinkable {the 4: A II 80}

***accantasaṃyoga**—(gram. term) direct governance (of acc. by transitive verb): M-a I 15; Khp-a 106

***accādhāya**—(ger. *ati* + *ādahati*) overlapping: M I 274

***accukkaṭṭha**—(*ati* + *u* + *kassati*) too high, too much pulled up (of robe): M II 139

***accokaṭṭha**—(*ati* + *ava* + *kassati*) too low (of robe): M II 139

***accosāna**—*see*: *abyosāna*

acchariya-dhamma—marvellous idea <or quality> {the 4: M-a III 365}

***acchādi**—covering sheath (*anacchādikata*): Khp.49

***acchādeti**—*also* to sustain (life or comfort), to be agreeable to the palate: M I 275, 316; D III 85; *see*: *chādeti*

***acchinna**—*also* new, not yet cut up (of cloth): Vin I 306

***accheda**—aor. caus. of *chindati*

***ajata**—limitless (?): Vism-a 323

***ajjattanī**—(gram.) aorist tense

ajjhatta—internally, in oneself {4 kinds: *gocarajjhatta* (in oneself as resort); *niyakajjhatta* (in oneself as one's own); *ajjhattajjhatta* (in oneself as such); *visayajjhatta* (in oneself as objective field): Dhs-a 46}

***ajjhājīva**—(*adhi* + *ājīva*) concerning livelihood: M II 245

***ajjhāropeti**—(*adhi* + *ā* + *ruhati*, caus.) to superimpose: New Sub-comy. to DN 1

ajjhāsaya—inclination, bent {2 kinds: *vipann-* and *sampann-*: Vism-a 112; 6 kinds: Vism 116}

ajjhāsayānusandhi—*see*: *anusandhi*

***ajjhāharati**—to adduce, add, supply: Khuddas

ajjhupekkhati—to look on at

***ajjhottharamāna**—*also* threatening: Vism 187

ajjhosita—accepted (by affirmation), <held on to>

***añcita**—outstretched: Vism 635; Vibh-a 454 (= *gata*: Vibh-mṭ)

***añjita**—*see*: *añcita*

aññā—(fr. *ājānāti*) final knowledge (of the Arahant)

***aññāti**—to know (= *ājānāti*): Paṭis I 122

aññā-vyākaraṇa—declaration of final knowledge {5 kinds: A III 119}

***aṭṭhaka**—(*ā*+ *ṭhā*+ *ka*) standing on: Vibh-a 519

aṭṭhaka—(material) octad: Vism 341, 364, 560, 588

aṭṭhaṅgika-magga—eightfold path

***aṭṭhadantaka**—harrow, rake: A-a 394

***aṇati**—*see: anati* (in exegesis of *brāhmaṇa*): M-a I 109

***aṇimā**—minuteness: Vism 211

aṇu—atom, minute measure (36 *paramāṇu* = 1 a.; 36 a. = 1 *tajjārī*: Vibh-a 343)

***atammayatā**—(*a* + *taṃ*+ *maya* + *tā*) lit. "not-belonging-to-that-ness," aloofness, absence of craving, <non-identification>: M III 42, 220 (cf. *tammaya*: M I 318)

aticchatā— = *atricchatā* [def. Vibh 350]

***atidesa**—extension (of meaning) (gram.)

***atināmeti**—to upset the proportion, to exceed: M II 138

***atinijjhāyitatta**—state of over-pondering, over-illumination, <excessive contemplation>: M III 160

***atipāteti**—to surpass: M I 82, S I 62

***atippasaṅga**—over-generalization (log.): Vism 472

atimāna—pride [def. M-a I 170]

***atisāra**—bowel, flux, diarrhoea: Vism 345

***atiharaṇa**—*also* shifting forward: M-a I 260; Vism 622

atīta—past, bygone

atīta-kāla—past tense (gram.)

***atula**—unjudgeable: M I 386

***attajjhāsaya**—(sutta given) to suit the speaker's inclination (one of the 4 kinds of *sutta-nikkhepa*, q.v.)

***attatā**—selfness, selfhood, individual self state: Vism 308

***attanopada**—middle (reflexive) voice of verb (gram.)

***attaparibhava**—self-despising: Vibh-a 486

attabhāva—person (the physical-mental personality), individuality, <body>

*__attavaññā__—self-contempt: Vibh-a 486

*__attavant__—possessed of a self, having an individual self: Paṭis-a362

attavāda—self-theory

attā—self [def. D I 192; II 64; M I 138; III 282; S III 46, 66]

attānudiṭṭhi—self-view, (wrong) view that self exists

*__attānuvāda__—self-reproach: Vism 222

*__attuññā__—self-depreciation: Vibh-a 486

attha—(1) benefit, good, (2) meaning, (3) purpose, aim, goal, need

atthaṅgama—subsidence, disappearance {2 kinds: *khaṇik-* (momentary) and *paccay-* (due to subsidence of the condition): M-a II 11}

*__atthabbana-veda__—the Atharva Veda: Vism-a 239

*__atthayati__—to be needed: Vism 98

atthi—to be there, there is, exists

atthika—seeking, <in need of>

*__atthikatā__—(*atthika-tā*) state of seeking, <in need of, needing>: Vism 466

atthikaroti—to heed, to be aware of

atthita-vata—no ordinary (?); (reading?): M II 212

*__atthin__— = *atthika*: Sn 957; Mv 37:166; 37:173

*__atthuppatti__—(preaching of a sutta) owing to a need arisen (one of the 4 kinds of *sutta-nikkhepa*, q.v.)

atricchatā—ambition, excessiveness of wishes (*see*: *aticchatā*)

*__athabbana-veda__—the Atharva Veda: M-a III 362

adiṭṭha—unseen

adinnādāna—taking what is not given, stealing

*__adīyati__—senses, feels (= *vedeti*): M-a III 362

adukkhamasukha—neither-pain-nor-pleasure, neither-painful-nor-pleasant

*__adūhala__—trap, snare: A-a 22 (?)

adosa—non-hate [def. Dhs 33; Vism 465]

***adduva (aḍḍuva?)**—knee (= *jaṇṇuka*): M II 137

addhā, addhāna—period, extent (time or space)

adharāraṇī—lower fire-kindling stick: Vism 489

***adhika**—*also* apart, away from: Vism-a 446

***adhikaraṇa**—(1) container: Dhs-a 61; M-a I 9; (2) causative voice of verb (gram.); (3) one kind of the locative case in the sense of containing (gram.)

***adhikaraṇa**—(adv.) because of: M I 86; Vibh 390. cf. *adhikicca*

***adhikāra**—subject-matter, treatise, heading: Vism 117; Dhs-a 58; Khp-a 112,113; M-a I 151

***adhikicca**—on account of (ger. *adhikaroti* used as adv.): Vibh-a 143; serving as: Vism 450

***adhigaccha**—(adv. = *adhigamma*) on account of: Vibh 325

***adhigata**—position, attitude to: S III 46,130 <but from D III 249 and A III 292 it seems that *avigata* is the correct reading>

adhigama—approach (approach to scripture), arrival: Khp-a 39; M-a I 6

***adhigama**—*also* "scribing" (of "scripture"): Khp-a 103; M-a I 6

adhicitta—the higher cognizance, higher consciousness or mind (= term for *jhāna*)

***adhiṭṭhāna**—(1) foundation; (2) steadying (of mind); (3) resolve

***adhiṭṭhāna**—*also* habitat: Vism 331, 463

***adhiṭṭhāna**—in terms of (i.e., sutta expressed in terms of e.g., elements): M-a I 24

adhipaññā—understanding connected with the path, higher understanding

adhipati—dominance, predominance {the 4: Vibh 216}

adhipateyya—dominance, predominance

***adhipāṭimokkha**—concerning the Code of Rules (*Pātimokkha*): M II 245 (not as in PED)

adhippāya—purport, intent
adhimuccati—to decide, <to resolve on>
adhimutta—decided, <resolved>
adhimutti—decision, <resolve> {2 kinds: *hīn-* (inferior) and *paṇīt-* (superior)} : Vism-a 198 [def. Vibh 340]
adhimokkha—decision, <resolution> [def. Vibh 165]
***adhirājā**—viceroy (?): Dhp-a Epil.
adhivacana—designation
***adhisayati**—to lie on: M I 173
***adhisallikhatar**—too much of an effacer, <too exacting>: M I 449
adhisīla—the higher virtue, virtue connected with jhāna or path
***adhīta**—(pp. of *dhīyati*) studied, learnt: Vism-a
anaggha—invaluable {4 kinds: Dhp-a III 120}
anaññātaññassāmītindriya—the I-shall-come-to-know-the-unknown faculty
***anati**—(1) to bring (= *āvahati*): M-a III 443 (see *aṇati*); (2) to breathe: Khp-a 124
anati—non-inclination
anattā—not-self (*-lakkhaṇa-kāraṇa*, reason for the characteristic of n-s, the 4: M-a II 113) [def. M I 138; III 282; S III 66]
anantavant—infinite, endless
***anapāya**—(*an* + *apa* + *i*) not retreating from: M III 25
***anaya**—(*a* + *naya*) wrong way: M-a I
anaya—(*an* + *aya*) calamity
***anala**—fire: Vism-a (to Vism 507-8)
anāgata—future
anāgataṃsa-ñāṇa—knowledge of the future`
anāgata-kāla—future tense (gram.)
anāgāmin—non-returner (3rd stage of realization)

anicca—impermanent (*-lakkhaṇa-kāraṇa*, reason for the characteristic of imp., the 4: M-a II 113)

*__aniñja__—imperturbable: Vibh-a 144

aniñjana—non-perturbation

anidassana—invisible, that makes no showing

anipphanna—unproduced (see *nipphanna*); *-rūpa* {10 kinds.: Abhi-av 74}

animitta—signless

aniyata—uncertain, variable, unfixed

aniyāmita—indefinite (relative pronoun, e.g., *yaṃ*) (gram.)

*__anīlaka__—pure, unsullied (= *nimmakkhika, parisuddha*: Vin-a 18): Vin III 7

anukampā—compassion, pity {2 kinds: A I 92}

*__anugati__—*also* form of belief, tenet: M I 16

*__anugamana__—(1) inference, conclusion, form of belief: Vism 643; (2) positive (opp. of *byatireka*) (log.): Vism-a

anuggaha—compassion, help {2 kinds: It 98}

*__anuggahita__—taken up: Paṭis I 160

*__anucara__—governor: Dhp 294

*__anuṭṭhāna__—(*anu* + *ṭhāna*) maintenance: Khp-a 229

*__anutthunana__—brooding, mourning: Vism 506

anudhamma—adapted in idea to, according to dhamma

anunaya—approval

anuparivattati—to turn over parallel with, <to occur along with> Dhs 5; Dhs-a 49

anuparivatti—having parallel turn-over with, <occurring along with> Dhs 1522

an-upalabbhamāna, anupalabbhanīya—impossible, self-contradictory, unfindable, non-existent (log.)

*__anupavesati__—*also* to interfere with: Vism-a 364

anupassati—to contemplate

anupassanā—contemplation {3 kinds: Paṭis I 58; 7 kinds: Vism 289, 658; 44 kinds: M-a I}

anupādisesa—without result of past clinging left (a term for *nibbāna* at demise of Arahant)

*__an-upāya__—(*an* + *upa* + *i*) not approaching: M III 25

anupālana—maintenance, upkeep, protection

*__anupubbikathā__—*also* previous history: M-a II 19; III 328; V 85

anuppabandhana—anchoring, keeping tied down (description of *vicāra*): Vism 142

*__anuppīyabhāṇitā__—ingratiating chatter: Vibh 352

*__anubuddhi__—conviction, certainty, discovery owed to another: M-a II 386; V 105

anubodha—conviction, certainty, discovery owed to another (causative form)

anubhāva—might, influence

*__anubhūta__—*also* coessential with, <commensurate with> (*an-*): M I 329

anumāna—inference

*__anumāssa anumāssa__—point by point: M I 146 <but correct reading should be: *anumassa anumassa*>

*__anuyoga__—*also* corollary: Kv 56

anuloma—conformity (knowledge) {3 kinds: Vism 669-70; Paṭṭh 159}

anuvahanā—continuous following: Vism 278

*__anuvicarāpeti__—to make walk all round, to explore: M I 253

*__anuvicāreti__—to meditate: M II 253

*__anusaṭa__—(pp. of *anuseti*?) underlain by: Vism 232; Paṭis I 127 (see Paṭis-a280-81)

anusandhi—sequence of meaning in a sutta {3 kinds: *pucch-* (s-o-m based on a question asked); *ajjhāsay-* (s-o-m dictated by another's inclination); *yath-* (s-o-m dictated by the natural course of the Dhamma): M-a I 175}

anusaya—underlying tendency {the 7: M I 109-10; S IV 41; Vibh 383} [def. Vism 684; Vism-a 197]

*__anusāveti__—to proclaim: M-a IV 112; Vin II 203

***anusāvana**—proclamation: Vin II 85

***anusvāra**—nasal consonant, *niggahīta* (gram.)

anussati—recollection (the 10)

***anekattha**—suffix (gram.)

***anekantikatā**—inconclusiveness, over-generalization (log.)

***aneñja, aneja**—unperturbed: Paṭis II 206; Vism 386

anesanā—improper search: M-a I 115 {21 kinds: Khp-a 236}

***anogāḷha**—unfathomed (-*paññā*—wisdom): M-a I 292

anottappa—shamelessness, <fearlessness of wrongdoing, moral recklessness>

***antarakappa**—<intermediary aeon> {3 kinds: Vism-a 415}

antaradhāna—disappearance {3 kinds: M-a IV 115; 5 kinds: A-a to A I 42}

antarābhava—the (heretical notion of an) interval between existences: Ud-a 92-93

antarāyika-dhamma—obstructive idea <or state> {the 5: M-a III 102}

antavant—finite

***antokaraṇa**—the Inner Organ (as described in brahmanical philosophy = *antaḥkaraṇa*): Vism-a

***antokaraṇa**—appropriation: Dhs-a 48

***antokaroti**—to appropriate: Dhs-a 48

***andolika**—swinging seat: Khuddas-a 398 Be, Sp-ṭ III 294.

***andhandhaṃ**—darkly: M III 151

***anvakāsi**—(aor. of *anukassati* [?]) threw down into (= *khipi, chaḍḍesi*: M-a III 334): M II 100 <but M II 100 reads *anvakāri; anvakāsi* is from Th 869>

anvaya—necessity (*dhamm*- necessity of an idea <or principle>)

***anvaya**—*also* positive (opp. of *byatireka* = *anugamana*) (log.): Vism-a 580

anvaye ñāṇa—knowledge of necessity

***anvāgameti**—to allow to go, to revive, <to review>: M III 187

***anvāvaṭṭana**—(attention that) occurs parallel with, follows: M-a I 64

***apakaṭṭha**—worn loosely (of robes): M II 139

***apakassa**—*also* (ger. *apa* + *kas*?) shrinking back: S II 198

apacaya—dispersal

***apadāna—conduct (*bālāpadāna*—**fools' conduct: M-a IV 210): M III 163

***apanayana**—objection: M-a I 244

apariyāpanna—unincluded

***aparisaṇṭhita**—turbulent, unquiet: Vism 194

***apaloketi**—*also* to look away: M I 120

apavārita—(*apa* + *vārita*) opened up: Vism 178

***apasaddapayoga**—ungrammatical construction

***apassena**—(?): Khp-a 30

apāya—(1) state of deprivation or loss (the 4); (2) detriment: Vibh 326f.

apilāpanatā—state of non-drifting (in definition of *sati*) (but see Mil 37; M-a I 82)

***apekkha**—*also* passion, interest: M II 223

appa—few, little {4 kinds: A II 26}

***appaccattha**—suffix (gram.)

appaṭigha—without resistance, <not impinging on senses>

***appaṭivibhatta**—not sharing impartially: M I 322; M-a II 396

appaṇihita—desireless, not looking to something superior

appanā—fixing, absorption: M III 73 (no sutta ref. in PED)

***appanā**—conclusion (in argument): M-a II 30; Dhs-a 55; Vibh-a 401

***appabaddha**—unhesitant: M I 213

appamaññā—measureless state (the four: = divine abidings)

appamāṇa—measureless

appamāda—diligence

***appāyati**—to satisfy (in exegesis of *āpo*): Vism 364; Vibh-a 9

appiccha—of few wishes {4 kinds: A-a }

appicchatā—(*appa* + *icchā* + *tā*) fewness of wishes {4-fold: Sn-a to Sn 707}

***appita**—done away with: Vibh 258; Vism 157

appita—absorbed, fixed: Vibh 195

***aphassita**—uncontacted: M I 475 (cf. PED *phassita*)

***abbokāra**—(*a* + *vokāra*) not mixing: Vibh-a 51

abbokiṇṇa—consecutive, continuous

abbohārika—negligible, can be disregarded

***abbyāhati**—to draw out: M II 216 (reading?)

***abbhaṅga**—unguent: Vism 29

***abbhantara**—measure of length (4 *yaṭṭhi* = 1 a.; also 28 *hattha* = 1 a.; 4 a. = 1 *usabha*)

***abbhāhata**—buffeted, shaken: Vism 279 (cf. *samabbhāhata*)

***abbhutita**—(*abbhuṃ* + *ita*?) obscured: Vin-a 976

abbhussāhita—motivated, moved to: Khp-a 192

***abyabhicārin**—without exception (gram. and log.): Vism 441

abyāpāda—non-ill will

abyābajjha—non-affliction

***abyosāna**—not stopping half-way: Vism 613 (another reading is *accosāna*)

abrahmacariya—what is not the life divine <the holy life>, unchastity

abhāva—absence, non-entity, non-existence

***abhāva**—sexless: Vism 551

***abhāsati**—to transcend, to ward off (= *abhibhavati*, *paṭibāhati*): M-a V 20

***abhigacchati**—to rely on: Khp-a 81, 85; Vism 211

abhighāta—impact

abhijānāti—to know directly, to know definitely (either by "book-knowledge" or by experience)

abhijjhā—covetousness [def. Vibh 252]: M-a I 169

*__abhijjhāna__—coveting: M-a IV 58

abhiññā—(1) direct knowledge; (2) knowledge of supernormal success (the 5 kinds and 6 kinds)

abhito—(adv.) near: M I 338; no sutta ref. in PED

*__abhidhāna__—act of naming (gram.)

*__abhidheyya__—thing named (gram.)

abhinandati—to relish, <to delight in>

abhinandana—act of relishing, <delighting in> {5 kinds: Vism 514; Vism-a 208}

abhinipāta—engagement, conjunction

*__abhinipphajjati__—to be produced: M I 86

*__abhinipphanna__—produced: M II 225

abhiniropana—act of directing on to (exegesis of *saṅkappa*)

*__abhinivisati__—*also* to interpret, to misinterpret, to insist upon (either rightly or wrongly): M-a II 338; Vism 661 (ger. *abhinivissa*: M I 136; III 210)

*__abhinivesa__—*also* insistence: M I 73,136; interpretation: M-a I 276; Vism 462; misinterpretation: M I 136

*__abhinīhāra__—*also* conveying: Vism 365, 411; guidance: Paṭis I 17; I 61

abhibhavati—to be transcendent, to transcend, to overcome

abhibhāyatana—base for transcending (form) (the 8: D II 110)

abhibhū—the Transcender, the Transcendent Being (brahmanical?): name for one of the Brahmā gods

abhimata—outstanding

*__abhimāna__—assumption: Vism-a 467

*__abhiyuñjana__—act of entering: Khuddas-a 11-12

*__abhiyuñjeti__—to enter: Khuddas-a 11-12

abhivadati—(1) to welcome, to praise; (2) to affirm

*__abhividhi__—restriction (gram.)

*__abhivyatti__—particular distinction: *anuṭīkā* to DN Sutta 1

***abhisaṃharati**—to make a profit: Vism 312; to bring together: Vibh-a 6

abhisaṅkharoti—to determine, <to form>

abhisaṅkhāra—determination, <formation> {the 3: S II 58}

abhisañcetayita—involving exercise of will or volition

abhisañceteti—to will, to exercise volition

abhisandana—act of moistening

abhisandahati—to collect (in exegesis of *cetanā*): Vism 463; Dhs-a 111

***abhisandhi**—(*sābhisandhika*) preparation: M-a V 16

abhisamaya—penetration to, arrival at, convergence {2 kinds: Vism 216}

***abhihaṭṭhuṃ**—(inf.) to allow to be brought (*abhihaṭṭhuṃ pavāreti*: invites to have (robes, etc.) brought and accepted): M I 222 (= *abhiharitvā pavāreti*, M-a II 264; cf. Vin Nissaggiya-pācittiya no. 7) PED does not agree

abhihāra—bringing of offerings {2 kinds: M-a II 264}

amata—deathless (term for *nibbāna*)

amanasikāra—non-attention

***amarā**—(explained by M-a as aor. of *marati*): M II 73; (explained by Th-a as nom. pl. of adj. *amara*): Th 779

amoha—non-delusion [def. Dhs 34; Vism 465]

***ambaṇa**—kind of coin (*kahāpana-nāmaṃ*): Vibh-a 519

***ambilaka**—tamarind: A-a

aya—way

***aya**—*also* reason, source: Vism 427 (in exegesis of *apāya*); way to pleasure: Vism 495

***ayakanta-pāsāṇa**—lodestone, magnet: M-a V 87

***ayita**—(pp. of *eti*?) gone to (?): Vibh-a 75

ayoni—no reason: M III 141; no Piṭaka ref. in PED

ayoniso—(adv.) a. *manasikāra*: unreasoned <unwise> attention

***araṇa**—non-conflict: M III 235

***araṇīya**—(absol. of *ariyati*) to be served, to be honoured: Khp-a 81, 236; M-a I 21, 173 (= *payirūpāsitabba*: MA-a.); Vibh-a 386

arati—boredom, non-delight [def. Vibh 352]

***arahati**—*also* to be likely: Vin I 278; to be fitting: M II 165

arahant—arahant, accomplished one (4th and final stage of realization) [def. Vism 198]

***ariṭṭha**—kind of thorny tree with fruits: M-a IV 136; Vism 249; Vism-a

ariya—noble (*-puggala*) {the 7: Vism 659} [def. M-a I 21]

***ariyati**—to be served, to be honoured: Vism 440 (CPD has "to approach")

ariya-vaṃsa—noble ones' heritage {the 4: A II 27}

arūpa—formless, <immaterial>

arūpa-dhātu—formless <immaterial> element

arūpa-bhava—formless <immaterial> being

arūpa-loka—formless <immaterial> world (Vism 511, 548)

arūpāvacara—formless <immaterial> sphere

alabbhamāna—impossible, self-contradictory (log. = *anupalabbhanīya*)

***aluta**—inestimable: M I 386

alobha—non-greed [def. Dhs 32; Vism 465]

***allīna**—(*ā* + *līyati*) relied on for shelter (see PED *leṇa*): Vism 217

***allīna**—(*a* + *līyati*) unsheltered: Vism 612

***avakaṃsato**—(adv.) at the minimum: Vism 552

***avakāri**—analysis (= *vinibbhoga*): Vibh 393

***avakhaṇḍana**—hiatus: Vism 60

***avagata**—descended into (only uncertain reading in PED: Khp-a 15)

***avagantar**—(m.) a descender into: Khp-a 135

***avagāha**—grasping (= *ogāha*): Vism 516

***avacāreti**—to be occupied with: Vibh-a 144

***avacchinna**—separated (?): Vism-a 814

***avaṭṭhāyi**—(*kālantara*) lasting for a time: Vism-a to Vism 629

***avatthapīyati**—to be settled on (gloss for *avadhāna*): Paṭis-a8

***avatthā**—occasion, opportunity, position: Vism 161, 584, 612

***avatthāpana**—act of defining: Paṭis II 21

***avatthāpeti**—to make defined: Paṭis II 38

***avatthika**—defined (*svāvatthika*: well defined): Paṭis II 38

***avadāriyati**—to dig, to break up (gloss for *khaṇati*): Abh

***avadisati**—to point out: M-a I 92

***avadhāna**—application (*sotāvadhāna*: applying or lending the ear): M II 175; Paṭis I 1 (cf. *ohita-sota*)

***avadhāraṇa**—*also* memorizing: M-a I 3-4; Khp-a 100

***avadhi**—limit, limitation: Vism 31 (= *odhi*) {2 kinds: *abhividhivisayo avadhi* and *anabhividhivisayo avadhi*: As-mṭ 51}

***avadhīyati**—to learn about: Paṭis-a8

avabodha—awareness, discovery

avayava—constituent (of compound) (gram.)

***avarodha**—inclusion: Vism 478; Vibh-a 31

***avaloketi**—to survey, to look back at (= *oloketi*): D II 96; M II 137

***avassaṃ**—*also* without fail (adv.): M-a II 67

***avāsa**—non-residence, eviction: Vism 120

***avi**—goat or sheep: Vism 543

avikkhepa—non-distraction (function of *samādhi*) [def. Dhs 57]

avijjā—ignorance, nescience, unknowing {4 kinds: Dhs-a 51} [def. Dhs 1152; Vibh 85, 135; Vism 528]

***avisārī**—decisive, musical, not discordant (of voice): M II 140

***avyaya**—indeclinable adverb (gram.)

avyayībhāva—adverbial compound (gram.)

***avyākata**—(1) undeclared (i.e., in the first triad of the Abhidhamma Mātikā = "not called either *kusala* or *akusala*," "morally undeclared"); (2) undeclared, unanswered (i.e., the 10 or 14 types of question unanswered by the Buddha)

avyāpāda—non-ill will (= *abyāpāda*)

***avyāya-taddhita**—indeclinable numeral as adverb (gram.)

***asa**—(*as'asmi*) eternal (*tattha atthī ti asa; niccass' etaṃ adhivacanaṃ*: Vibh-a 514): Vibh 392

asaṅkhata—undetermined, <unformed, unconditioned> (term for *nibbāna*) [def. M III 63; S iv.359f.; A I 152]

asaṅkhāra, asaṅkhārika—unprompted

***asajjamāna**—*also* unhesitating: Vism 635

asaññin—non-percipient

***asati**—to reap, to cut: MA-a.

asani—thunderbolt {9 kinds: D-a 569}

***asabhāvadhamma**—an idea <or state> (*dhamma*) with no individual essence (e.g., *paññatti, nirodha-samāpatti, ākāsa, aniccatā, vikāra-rūpa*, etc.):

***asamāhāra**—*dvandva* compound with plural termination (gram.)

asammoha—non-confusion, non-delusion

***asita**—reaped, cut (*asitabyābaṅgin*): M II 180; Vibh-a 515

asubha—foul, ugly, foulness, ugliness

asekha—an adept, <one beyond training> (= an arahant)

asmi-māna—the conceit "(I) am"

***assati**—to abandon (= *nirassati, pajahati*): Vism-a 135; A-a

assāda—gratification, <attraction, enjoyment>

***assādeti**—*also* to like, to be attracted by: Vism 554

***assāvi**—*also* discharging (of wound): M II 257

assāsa-passāsa—in-breath and out-breath

***assu**—aor. 2nd pers. sing. of *suṇāti* (see under *suṇāti* in PED): M I 228

assutavant—untaught

***ahata**—new (of cloth): M-a IV 187

ahirājakula—family of royal (serpents): {the 4: A II 72}

ahirika—consciencelessness, <shamelessness>

***ahu**—aor. 3rd pers. sing. of *hoti*: M I 376, 403, 487; II 51; A I 197

ahetu—non-reason, non-cause

ahetuka—(1) without reason, without cause; (2) (consciousness) unaccompanied by *hetu*; q.v. *hetu* (2): Vism 454-55

ahetuka-diṭṭhi—view that nothing has a reason, cause

ahetuka-vāda—theory that nothing has a reason, cause

***aho-ratta**—day and night: M I 98; III 294

***ahosi-kamma**—lapsed kamma (i.e., kamma that has been performed and has not and will not have ripening): Vism 601 (see Paṭis II 78)

Ā

***ākara**—*also* store, <mine>: Vism 482

***ākallaka**—sick: Khuddas

***ā-kāra**—the prefix *ā-* (*kāra* = syllable): M-a I 61 (gram.)

ākāra—mode, aspect, evidence {the 32: Vism 240} Khp.2

***ākāra**—derivative verbal noun ending in *-ana* (gram.)

***ākāra-rūpa**—form as mode (e.g., mark of the female, etc.): Vism

***ākāra-vikāra**—mode-alteration (e.g., *aniccatā, viññatti*): Vism 448

ākāsa—space [def. M I 423; Dhs 638; Vibh 84]

ākāsānañcāyatana—base consisting of infinity of space (1st of the 4 *āruppa*)

ākiñcañña—nothingness

ākiñcaññāyatana—base consisting of nothingness (3rd of the 4 *āruppa*)

***ākulayati**—(caus. fr. *ākula*) to mix up: Vism-a 106
***ākhyāta**—verb (gram.)
āgama—"scripture," body of texts handed down: M-a I 6; Khp-a 39
āgamana—act of coming to
āgamanīya—according to the way of arrival (at the path): M-a II 367
āgamma—(ger. of *gam*) (1) having come to; (2) owing to, <dependent on> (adv.)
āghāta—annoyance
ācaya—setting up (one of the kinds of *upādā-rūpa*)
ācariya—teacher {3 kinds: *Gandhavaṃsa*}
***ācariyaka**—*also* teachers' doctrine: M I 164; II 32
***ājānāti**—*also* to acknowledge: Kv 1
ājīva—livelihood [def. Vibh 105,107; Vism 510]
ājīvaṭṭhamaka—with livelihood as eighth: Vism 11; Vism-a 28; M-a II 387
ātapatappana—mortification {5 kinds: M-a II 11}
***ātapa-pattaka**—(palm)-leaf sunshade: Khuddas 74
ādāna—act of grasping (*sārādāna* = grasping at a core [of permanence, etc.])
ādi—(1) beginning; (2) et cetera (encl.): *ti ādisu* (after quotation) = "in such passages as"; *ti ādi* (after quotation) = "in the passage beginning"; *ti ādinā nayena* (after quotation) = "in the way beginning thus"
***ādissa**—(adj. *ādisati*) reproachable: M I 12 (see PED *Corrigenda*)
***ādīna**—wretched: Vism 612
ādīnava—inadequacy, danger, disability, disadvantage {5 kinds: Vibh 378}
***ādhāna (ādāna)**—lighting: A IV 41
ādhāra—support to stand something on
***ādhāra**—the locative case (gram.)

***ādhāraka**—*also* a parcel (?): Vibh-a 448

***ādhāraṇa**—upholding, subserving: M-a II 52; Vism 447

***ādhīyati**—to be collected (gloss of *samādhi*): M-a I 174

***ādhunika**—from the start (-neyya = to be guided from the start)

ānantarika—(action) with immediate result after death {5 kinds: Vibh 378; M-a II 102; IV 110}

ānāpāna—breathing, inhalation-exhalation

***ānīta**—(*-pañhā*) leading question: M-a II 292

ānuttariya—unsurpassable (the 4)

āneñja—imperturbability (term for the 4th jhāna and the *āruppa* attainments)

āpajjati—to enter upon

***āpajjati**—*also* to follow logically (loc.): Vism 80, 507

***āpajjana**—(undesirable) logical consequence (log.): Vism 507

***āpaṇika**—from a shop (= *pāpaṇika*): Vibh-a 480; Vin III 64

***āpatti**—also = *āpajjana*: Vism 509

āpatti—offence (against Vinaya rules) {5 *āpatti-kkhandha*: Dhs-a 7, 52; M-a II 33}

***āpātaparipāta**—fall on and around: Ud 72

āpātha—threshold (of door to consciousness), range, focus, horizon

***āpādana**—production: Vism 64; Vibh-a 102

***āpādikā**—nurse: M III 253

***āpādetar**—nurse: M III 248

āpo—water (as element), liquidness [def. M I 422; Dhs 652; Vism 350, 351-52, 353, 363, 365; Vism-a 359; Vibh 83]

***ābaddha**—*also* belonging to (*nānābaddha* belonging to many; *ekābaddha* a man's own): Vism 706

ābandhana—cohesion (exegesis of *āpo-dhātu*)

ābādha—affliction

***ābhañjati**—to lean upon (= *olambati* in exegesis of *asitabyābaṅgin* at M II 180): M-ṭ III 197

ābhoga—concern (the mind's concern with a special aspect)

***āmaṇḍa**—gall-nut (= *āmalaka*): M III 101

āmantā—(expression of assent) "agreed": Kv 4; Yam.

āmisa—material, <worldly, bait> {2 kinds: M-a I 89; 3 kinds: Vibh-a 421; Vism 650}

āmeṇḍita—reduplicated (word) (gram.): M-a II 127

āya—improvement: Vism 427

***āyatati**—to range over (to activate?): Vism 481; cf. Paṭis II 20

āyatana—base (range) for contact (the 6 in oneself <internal>/external) [def. Vism 481,528]

***āyatana**—*also* opportunity: M III 96; act of ranging over (actuating?): Vism 481

***āyatika**—based on (*kusal-*): M III 115

***āyana**—way, act of going: Vism 26

***āyava**—*see*: *āsava*

āyu—life-span, life

āyu-saṅkhāra—vital determination, <formation> (= *usmā* and *āyu*)

āyūhana—accumulation (of kamma)

***āyūhita**—accumulated (kamma): M-a V 55

ārati—refraining (*ārati virati*): M III 74; no sutta ref. in PED

ārabbha—(ger. as adv.) contingent upon, owing to

***āramaṇa**—act of shunning: Khp-a 142

ārambha-vatthu—ground for initiative {the 8: D-a 530}

ārammaṇa—objective support, object {2 kds: Vibh-a 403; 4 kds: Vibh 332}

āruppa—formless, <immaterial> states (the 4)

***āropita**—strung (of a bow): Vism 72

***āropeti**—*also* to attribute to: Vism 618; M-a I 73

***ārohati**—to climb, to cast back to: Vism 422

***ālapana**—*also* vocative case (gram.)

ālaya—reliance, thing relied on
***ālasiya**—indolence: M-a III 145,181; Vibh 352 (cf. PED *alasi*)
āloka—light
***ālocita**—illuminated: Vism-a 851
āḷhaka—measure of volume (1 a. = 4 *pattha*)
āvajjana—adverting (of consciousness: first member of *cittavīthi*)
***āvatthā**—occasion, point: Vism-a 478
***āvatthika**—(name) denoting a period or occasion: Vism 209
***āviñchati (āviñjati)**—to move towards: Vibh-a ; As-mṭ 137 (*āviñchana*)
***āviñjana**—picking up (see PED *āvijjhati*), dealing with, directing towards: Vism 444; As-mṭ 137
āsatti—clutching, attachment
***āsana**—*also* altar: Vism 173
āsaya—(1) bias; (2) abode, physical basis: Khp-a 39; M-a I 6 {4 kinds: Vism 344; Vism-a 197}; (3) purpose
***āsarati**—to approach: Vibh-a 493
āsava—canker, taint {2 kinds: Vin III 21; 3 kinds: M I 55; 4 kinds: Vibh 373; 5 kinds: Vibh-a } [def. Vism 683; Dhs-a 48; M-a I 61]
***āsava (āyava, āsāva)**—energy (= *viriya*): Paṭis I 107
āsivisa—snake poison {4 kinds: A II 110; many kinds: S-a III 8}
***āsevanā**—repetition, cultivation
***āhañchaṃ**—fut. 1st pers. sing. of *āhanati*: M I 171
āhattar—bringer: M II 123
***āhanana**—striking at: Vism 142
āhāra—(1) nutriment; (2) quotation: Kv 69 {3 kinds: Vibh 405; 4 kinds: M I 48; A IV 106; another four kinds: Khp-a 207} [def. M I 47; Vism 341]
āhāra-samuṭṭhāna—having nutriment as origin, nutriment-originated (form)

I - Ī

icchatā—state of having wishes {4 kinds: M-a II 138}
icchati—to wish
***icchati**—to stir: M I 189 (see PED *aticchati*)
icchā—wish
iñjita—perturbation {the 9: Vibh 390}
***itarathā**—(adv.) otherwise: Vism 96; Dhs-a 44; M-a II 51
itthambhūta-vacana—ablative of likeness (gram.)
itthi—woman, female {the 9: M I 286; the 10: Vin III 138; M-a I 199}
itthindriya—femininity faculty
itthi-liṅga—feminine gender (gram.)
idappaccayatā—specific conditionality (= dependent origination)
iddhi—success, power, supernormal power {2 kinds: A I 93; 10 kinds: Paṭis II 205} [def. Vibh 217; Vism 670]
iddhi-pāda—basis for success, road to power (the 4) {8 *iddhiyā pāda*: Paṭis II 205-6} [def. Vibh-a 303f.]
iddhi-bala—power of success {the 10: Paṭis II 174}
iddhi-vidha—the kinds of supernormal success, power
***indana**—fuel: Vism 505; Vibh-a (a spelling of *indhana*)
indriya—faculty {2 kinds: S V 223; 3 kds: S V 204, 224; 4 kds: S V 223; 5 kds: S V 201, 211, 217; 6 kds: S V 205; 8 kds: Paṭis I 116; 22 kds: Vism 491} [def. Vism 491, 679]
iriyāpatha—posture, deportment {4 kinds: S V 78}
irubbeda—the Rig Veda: M-a III 362
***isati**—to shine: Ud-a 299
issara—overlord, <creator God>
issā—envy
īhaka—having curiosity, activity

U - Ū

***ukkaṃsato**—(adv.) at the maximum: Vism 552

***ukkaṭṭha**—(acc-) *also* hitched up (of robe): M II 139

***ukkara**—(*mūsik-*) thrown up (by rats): M II 51 (so read for *mūsikukkura*)

***ukkirati**—to paint (?): M-ṭ III 396

***ukkhaya**—ending (*niddukkhayavibuddha* = *niddā* + *ukkhaya* + *vibuddha*; probable misreading for *niddākkhaya-*): Khp-a 15

uggaha—learning

uggaha-nimitta—learning-sign (manifestation in contemplation)

ugghaṭita—condensed, abbreviated (opp. of *vipañcita*)

***ugghaṇita (ugghaṭita?)**—decayed: Vism 184

***ugghāta**—exhilarated: Vism 370

***ugghāti**—removal: Vism 113

***ugghātita**—removed (of *kasiṇa* concept when entering upon 1st *āruppa*): Vism 134

***ugghātīyati**—to get agitated: M-a II 83

uccheda—cutting off, annihilation

uccheda-diṭṭhi—annihilation view

uju—straight, erect

ujukatā—rectitude

uṭṭaṇḍa (uddaṇḍa)—granary (?): Nidd I 67; Vibh-a 481

***uṭṭhāhika**—vigilant, active: M-a II 99

***uḍḍita**—caught up (glossed with *ullaṅghati*): Paṭis I 128

uṇha—heat

***uṇhīsa**—*also* capital of column (?): D II 184

utu—(1) temperature; (2) season; (3) climate {2 kinds: Vism 616; 3 kinds: Vism-a 258; 4 kinds: Vism-a 794; 6 kinds: Vism 621}

utu-samuṭṭhāna—temperature-originated (class of components of the form-aggregate, *rūpakkhandha*)

***uttama-purisa**—1st person (gram.)
***uttara**—*also* conclusion (log.): Vism-a to Vism 451; M-a V 83
***uttarāraṇi**—upper fire-stick: Vism 489
uttari manussa-dhamma—dhamma higher than the human state (= *jhānas, abhiññās, maggas*, etc.)
udaya—rise
udayabbaya—rise and fall (*see also*: *vaya*)
***udāharīyati**—to be uttered: Vism 481
***uddānato**—briefly (adv. = *saṅkhepato*): M-ṭ III 218
uddesa—summary, indication, indicative pronoun (gram.)
uddhacca—agitation [def. Dhs 429; Vibh 276; Vism 469]
uddhacca-kukkucca—agitation and worry [def. M I 275-76]
***uddharati**—*also* to derive (a meaning): M-a I 86; to adduce: Vibh-a 316
***uddhasta**—risen (*uddhaste aruṇe*—dawn having arisen): Vin II 236; A IV 205 (PED and Ee Vin have v.l. *uddhata*)
***uddhāra**—*also* derivation (*atth-* der. of meaning): M-a IV 74
***unnītaka**—led off (= *uggaṇhitvā nīto*: Paṭis-a): Paṭis I 129
***upakāri**—bastion: M I 86
***upakuṭṭha**—smallpox (?): Vism 569 (cf. *kuṭṭha*)
upakkilesa—imperfection, defilement
***upakkhittaka**—a convert: Paṭis II 196
upaga—passing on to (used of consciousness's linking at death with a new existence)
upacaya—growth (of *rūpa*)
***upacarita**—*also* used metaphorically: Vism-a 513
upacāra—(1) neighbourhood, precinct; (2) access concentration
***upacāra**—*also* metaphor (*phal-* metaphorical use of fruit's name for its cause): Vism 508, 521; (*kāraṇ-* metaphorical use of cause's name for its fruit): Vism 683 (= *sammuti* and *vohāra*: It-a to It 43)

*__upajjati__—(*upa* + *ajjati*) to get together, to obtain: Khp-a 223 (*upajjetabba*)

*__upaṭṭhāna__—*also* (1) establishment (= *paṭṭhāna* in that sense): Paṭis I 177; (2) appearance, manifestation: Paṭis I 1; Vism 645 {3 kinds: Paṭis I 58; 5 kinds: Khp-a 127}

upatthambhana—consolidating, stiffening up, supporting

*__upadussati__—to begrudge, to show hate for through envy: M III 204

upaddava—risk, undoing, <calamity> {3 kinds: M III 115; 4 kinds: M-a I 237}

*__upadhā__—pillow: M I 79

*__upadhāna__— = *upadhā*: M I 75

*__upadhāraṇa__—upholding, holding up, supporting: Vism 8, 51

upadhi—essential of existence, substrate of being {4 kinds: M-a II 112}

*__upanaya__—(1) inducement, on-leading; (2) application (of example in syllogism) (log.): Vism 217

*__upanayana__—(1) act of inducing; (2) applying (of example in syllogism) (log.): Vism 217, 449; Kv 3

upanāha—revenge, vengefulness [def. M-a I 169]

*__upanikkhitta-paññatti__—additive description (concept): Pp-a 173-74

upanidhā—comparison

upanidhā-paññatti—appositional (comparative) descriptive (concept): Pp-a 174

*__upanisinna-kathā__—form of discourse (*see*: *kathā*): Dhs-a 78; M-a III 30

upanissaya—decisive support {3 kinds: Vism 536}

upapatti—reappearance, rebirth

*__upapada-tappurisa__—verbal dependent derivative compound (gram.)

upapāramī—minor perfection {the 10: M-a III 22}

upabrūhaṇa—intensification (function of *sukha*): Vism 147, 148

***upabrūhayati**—to intensify: Vism

upabhuñjaka—user, experiencer

upayoga-vacana, upayoga—accusative case (gram.)

upalabbhati—to be possible, to be apprehendable (log.)

upalabbhamāna—possible, apprehendable (log.)

***upavadati**—*also* to assume (*abhimānena upavadati*): M-a IV 27

***upavicarati**—to approach (with the mind): M III 216

upavicāra—approach (by the mind)

***upasa**—prefixed vowel (gram.)

upasaṃharati—to connect (mentally), to associate (mentally)

upasaṃhita—(mentally) connected, associated

***upasagga**—relinquishment: Paṭis-a324

***upasagga**—prefix (gram.)

***upasaṅkamitar**—visitor: M I 72

***upasaṭṭhatā**—(*upa* + *saj* + *tā*) menacedness: Vism 612

upasama—stillness, peace

***upasamaya**—(*du-vūpasamaya* =) difficult to still: S V 114

upādā—secondary, accessory (derivative) [def. Dhs 596]

upādāna—(1) fuel; (2) clinging {2 kinds: M-a II 156; 4 kinds: M I 66} [def. Vism 569; Vibh 136, 375; Vism-a 184]

upādāna-kkhandha—aggregate affected by clinging (the 5) [def. M III 16f.; S III 47f., 58f.; Vism Ch. XIV]

upādāniya—provocative of clinging (derivative)

upādā-paññatti—accessory (derivative) description (concept)

upādā-rūpa—secondary form, accessory (derivative) form (i.e., accessory to the 4 *mahā-bhūta*); {24 kinds: Vism 444f.; 23 kinds: Dhs 596ff.}

upādi—liable to arise, liability to arising: M II 257; It 38 (*anupādisesa*); Dhs p. 2, §§1037, 1416 (*dhammā upādino*)

upādiṇṇa—clung-to (by kamma): M I 185; no sutta ref. in PED [def. Dhs 653]

upāya—(1) means; remedy: Vibh 326 {2 kinds: Nidd I 80} (*see*: *anaya*); (2) bias

upāyāsa—despair [def. Vibh 100; Vism 504]

upekkhā—onlooking, equanimity {2 kinds: M-a V 26; 3 kinds: S IV 235; 10 kinds: Vism 160} [def. Dhs 153; Vism 160, 167, 318; Vism-a 92]

uposatha—observance day (at full-moon and half-moon) {3 kinds: A I 205; Kkh 3; 9 kinds: Kkh 10} [def. M-a IV 75]

***uppajjati**—*also* to be tenable (as a proposition): M III 282

***uppaṭipāṭiya**—out of its order, out of place in succession (not as in PED): M-a V 52; Vibh-a 390

uppatti—appearance, arising, rebirth

***uppatti**—*see*: *nikkhepa*

uppatti-bhava—being as re-arising, rebirth-process becoming {3 kinds: Vism 514; 9 kinds: Vibh 137}

uppanna—arisen {4 kinds: M-a III 251f.; Dhs-a 66}

***uppalaka**—rending (*-vāta*): Vibh 84

uppāda—arising

***uppādika**—storm: M-a V 88

***ubbattana**—rubbing (gloss for *ucchādana*): Vism-a 70

***ubbhajati**—to hitch up (the robe): Khuddas 165

***ubbhaṭṭhaka**—(*ubbhaṃ* + *ṭha* + *ka*) constantly standing (one of the Nigaṇṭha mortifications): M I 92

ubhatobhāgavimutta—one liberated in both ways (i.e., one who has attained the 4 *āruppa*s and the fruition of arahantship) {5 kinds: M-a III 188}

***ummaṅga**—tunnel (?): Vibh-a 367

***uyyojaniya**—connected with dismissing: M III 111

***uyhati**—(pass. of *uddharati*) to be flooded (in gloss of *ogha*): Nidd I 146

***ulumpa**—boat, raft, float: D II 89

***ullikhāpeti**—having one's hair dressed: M II 61

usabha—measure of length (20 *yatthi*=1 u.; 80 u.=1 *gāvuta*)

ussada—prominence; (-*niraya*) prominent (hell) {16 kinds: Vism 300; Vism-a 296}

***ussaya**—(*puññ*-) heap (of merit): M-a I 51; (*vant*-) heap (of what is thrown up by ants: gloss of *vammīka*): M-a II 128

ussahati—to be active in

ussādeti—to extol

ussāha—activity

***ussedeti**—(*u* + *sedeti*) to steam: Vin-a 176

ussoḷhi—(n. fr. *ussahati*) activity, active involvement, active commitment

***uhadati**—to defecate

***ūkā**—*also* measure of length (7 *likhā* = 1 ū.; 7 ū. = 1 *dhaññamāsa*) (see PED *Corrigenda*)

***ūrunda**—large, spacious (of room): M III 238

***ūhana**—hitting upon: Vism 142

E

ekaggatā—unification (of mind), one-pointedness (synonym for *samādhi*) [def. Dhs 11]

***ekaṭṭha**—coefficient with: Paṭis I 33; M-a I 74 {2 kinds: *pahān*- = *dhammas* (ideas, <states>) coefficient with the *micchatta* abandoned, and *sahajāt*- (or *sahaj*-) = *dhammas* (ideas, <states>) coefficient with the *sammatta* conascent, at the path moment Paṭis-a94}

ekatta—(1) unity; (2) identity; (3) single state

***ekadesa**—(log.) *see under*: *desa*

***ekanāḷika (kathā)**—(a discourse) taking each word in a basic paragraph and explaining it (e.g., as MN Sutta 33): M-a II 258

***ekavacana**—singular (gram.)

***ekasesa**—(log.) *see under*: *desa*

***eta-parama**—that at most: M I 80; M-a III 3; Vism 478

***etāva**—this much (-*parama*: this much at most): M I 246

***eraṇa**—act of moving: Khuddas

***eva**—*also* (1) too, as well: Khp-a 32, 99; Vism ; (2) only: Khp-a 28 (this latter very commonly used)

evaṃ-dhammatā—ineluctable regularity (method of): Vism 585

esanā—search (not as in PED) {2 kinds: A I 93; 3 kinds: D III 216} *see also*: *anesanā*

O

***okappaniya**—believable: M I 249

okāsa—(1) location; (2) opportunity

***okāseti**—to scatter on: S IV 290; Vism 394; Vism-a 391

***okkaṭṭha**—let down too low (of robe): M II 139

***okkhandhati**—to descend into: M-a I 238; Vism 636

***ogaḷati**—to run downwards: Vism 260

***ogāḷha**—fathomed (*anogāḷhapañña*: having understanding that has not fathomed): M-a I 135

ogha—flood (the 4) [def. Vism 684]

ociṇṇa—*see*: *otiṇṇa*

ojaṭṭhamaka—octad (of form) with nutrition as eighth: Vism 341, 364, 588; Khp-a 72

ojā—nutritive-essence, nutrition, sap

***ojoharaṇa**—<removing of bodily vitality (by disease) (?)>: M-a IV (?)

***otāreti**—*also* to expound (a doctrine): Vism ; M-a II 250; Mv 37

***otiṇṇa (ociṇṇa)**—*also* convinced, successfully deceived: S I 79

ottappa—shame, <fear of wrongdoing, moral dread> [def. Dhs 31; Vism 464]

***oddeti**—to be burst open: S-a I 56

***odhasta**—placed ready (not as in PED): M I 124

***odhāpeti**—to cause to put down: A-a
***opakkamika**—due to striving (= *upakkama*): M II 218
***opaṇati**—to bargain down: M-a III 194
***opaṇavidhā (-viyā)**—bargaining: M-a III 194
opapātika—apparitional, of apparitional birth
***opārambha**—censurable: M II 113
***obhagga**—looped: Vism 258; Vibh-a 241
***obhañjati (obhujati)**—to loop, to coil: Vism 358; Vibh-a 62
obhāsa—light, lighting up, radiance
***omaññanā**—conceit of inferiority: Vibh 353
***omatta**—subordinate: Vism 622; M-a I 260; Vibh-a 354
***omāna**—*also* conceit of inferiority (= *lāmako heṭṭhā māno*: Vibh-a 486): Vibh 353; A III 445
***oruhati**—to come down, to descend, to dismount: Vism 144
***olayati**—Khuddas-a 343
oḷārika—gross
***ovaṭṭi**—(fem.) lip, brim (?), hem: M-a III 238
***ovaṭṭikasāra**—a valuable worthy of being kept in the *ovaṭṭikā* (cf. Sinh. *hasta sāra vastu*: a valuable to be carried to safety by hand, i.e., in case of fire): M-a 284, 292, 360
***ovaṭṭikā**—pouch (formed by twisting hem of waist-cloth): M-a II 322
***ovaṭṭha**—(pp. *ovassati*) rained down upon, showered down: Vism 360; Vin IV 38
***osāpeti**—to realize the actual facts: S I 79
***osāraṇa**—(*dhamm-*) investigation (of ideas <or states>): M-a III 30
***osāreti**—*also* to be drowned (*udakaṃ osāretvā*): Vibh-a 430
***ohanati (oharati?)**—to drag down, to engulf: Vibh-a 140
***ohārika**—active, activated (*sabbohārika-citta*: fully active cognizance): A-a III 317
***ohīḷanā**—self-detesting: Vibh-a 486
***ohīḷitatta**—self-detestation: Vibh-a 486

K

***ka**—(*ko*) *also* where?: M II 52, 155

kaṅka—crow: M I 364, 429; PED gives "heron," but this will not fit context

kaṅkhā—doubt

***kaccha**—*also* appointment (?): Vibh-a 256

kaṭatta—performedness (of kamma) (*kaṭattā*—owing to kamma's having been previously performed)

***kaṇḍūyati**—to tickle, <to itch>: Vism 260; Vibh-a 243

***kaṇṇikā**—fungus, mould: Vism 250

***kataka**—*also* water-clearing nut: Vism 254; M-a II 13

***kattā**—subject of verb (gram.)

***kattu-kāraka**—active voice of verb (gram.)

***kattu-sādhana**—derivation of word from agent, e.g., *socatī ti soko* (gram.)

kathā—talk {32 kinds of *tiracchāna*-: M-a III 222; 3 kinds of *kathā*: M-a II 258; III 30; 4 kinds: Khp-a 125}

kathāvatthu—(1) name of Abhidhamma book; (2) the ten instances of (profitable) talk: M I 145; M-a I 98

kanta—desired

kappa—aeon, age {2 kinds: Nidd I 97} [def. M-a II 125]

kappita—conjectured

kappiya—allowable

kabaliṅkārāhāra—physical nutriment, food

kampana—shaking, wavering

kamma—(1) action, deeds, kamma; (2) work {2 kinds: Vibh-a 410; 4 kinds: D III 230; Vin II 89; 5 kds: Vibh 378; 12 kds: Vism 601; Paṭis II 78; 16 kds: Vibh 358}

***kamma**—*also* object of verb (gram.)

***kamma-kāraka**—passive voice of verb (gram.)

***kamma-kāraṇa**—torture {32 kinds: M-a II 116; Vism 499}

kammaññatā—wieldiness (of *kāya* and *citta*)

kammaṭṭhāna—place of work, meditation subject {2 kinds: Vism 97; 40 kinds: Vism 110}

***kamma-dhāraya**—adjectival compound (gram.)

kammanta—acts [def. Vibh 105-6; Vism 510]

kamma-patha—mode of action, course of action [def. Dhs-a 88; Vism 684]

kamma-bhava—being as action, kamma-process becoming

kamma-vaṭṭa—round of kamma {the 5: Vism 579}

kamma-vāda—theory that action is valid (= *kiriya-vāda*)

kamma-samuṭṭhāna—kamma-originated (form)

karaja—physical

karaṇa—(1) reason, cause; (2) act of doing

***karaṇa-vacana**—instrumental case

***karaṇa-sādhana**—derivation of word from instrumental sense (e.g., *etena socatī ti soko*)

karuṇā—compassion [def. Vibh 273; Vism 318]

***kala-bhāga**—a fractional part: M III 166

kalāpa—(1) group; (2) form-group (*aṭṭhaka, navaka* and *dasaka*)

***kalāpa-sammasana**—comprehension by groups (i.e., of the *khandhas* by the groups beginning with "*atīta*"): Vism 606

kalyāṇa—good (3 *kalyāṇatā*: Vism 147)

kalyāṇa-puthujjana—magnanimous ordinary man (i.e., one who has not attained a path but is practising for it): M-a I 40

kaviṭṭha—kind of fruit: A-a

***kasaṭa**—*also* dregs: M I 229; Paṭis II 86

kasāva—*see*: *kasāya* in PED

kasiṇa—(1) (adj.) whole (M I 328); (2) wholeness, totality, *kasiṇa* as a contemplation device {the 10: M II 14; Vism Chs. IV-V}

***kasimāna**—emaciation: M I 80

***kātara**—timid: M-a I 116

kāma—sensual desire, <sensual pleasure> (either the subjective defilement (*kilesa*) or the object of desire [*vatthu*]): Nidd I 1; cf. A III 410f. [def. Vibh 256; Nidd I 1; Dhs-a 62]

kāmaṃ—(adv.) of course, certainly, admittedly

kāma-guṇa—cords (strands) of sensual desire, <cords of sensual pleasure> (the 5): M I 85; cf. A III 411

kāma-cchanda—zeal for sensual desires, <sensual desire> [def. M I 275-76; Vism-a 137]

kāma-bhava—sensual-desire becoming; being or existence in the mode of sensual desires, <in the sensual-desire sphere> (i.e., with all 5 *indriyas* beginning with *cakkhu*)

kāma-rāga—lust for sensual desires, <for sensual pleasure>

kāmāvacara—(1) belonging to sensual-desire becoming (adj.); (2) the sensual-desire sphere (n.) (11-*loka*: A-a)

kāmesu micchācāra—misconduct in sensual desires

kāya—(1) body, group, order (of creatures); (2) body ([a] physical = *sarīra*, [b] mental = *nāma*); *see*: *rūpa*- and *nāma*- {2 kinds: Paṭis I 183} [def. Dhs-a 82]

***kāyati**—to talk (= *katheti*): Vism-a 101

kāya-sakkhin—body-witness (one who has attained all 8 *samāpatti* and any of the 4 paths or first 3 fruitions)

kāyānupassanā—contemplation of the body {the 14: M-a I 274}

kāra—syllable (gram.)

***kāraka**—*also* (*dukkara*-) performance (of difficult feats): M I 81

kāraka—doer

kāraṇa—(1) act of causing to do; (2) instrument; (3) cause, reason; (4) case, instance

kāla—time {4 kinds: A II 140} [def. Dhs-a 58]

***kāla**—tense (gram.)

***kālatthambha**—time-measuring post, solar time-piece: M-a I 122

***kālātipatti**—conditional derivative substantive (gram.)
kicca—function (*see also*: *buddha-kicca*)
kicca-rasa—nature as function (*see also*: *sampatti-rasa*)
***kiñcati**—to obstruct (?): M-a II 354
kiñcana—something, obstruction, owning: Ud-a 344; Vibh 368; *k.-palibodha*—impediment of owning: M-a I 27 {3 kinds: D III 217}
***kiñcanatā**—owning, ownership: M II 263; A I 206; II 177; III 170; Vism 654
***kiṇāti**—*also* to combat: Vism 318 (= *hiṃsati*)
***kittima-loha**—alloyed metal: Vibh-a 63 {3 kinds: M-ṭ I 73}
kimi—worm {32 kinds: Vism 258; 80 kinds: Vism 235}
***kirati**—to sprinkle: Vism 179
kiriya—(*-citta*) functional (consciousness or mind): Vism 456
kiriya-vatthu—example of action {3 kinds: Vism-a 135}
kiriya-vāda—theory that action is valid (= *kammavāda*)
kilesa—defilement (term for *taṇhā*, etc.) {10 kinds: Vism 683; 500 kinds: S-a I 187; 8 *kilesa-vatthu*: Vibh 385; 10 kinds: Vibh 341} [def. Vism 683]
***kisora**—foal: M II 153
ku—(prefix in sense of) bad (e.g., *kummagga—wrong road)
***kukata**—what is ill-done: Vism 470 (in exegesis of *kukkucca*)
***kukkuka**—*also* a plaintain tree that has not yet flowered: M I 233
kukkucca—worry [def. Vism 470]
***kuṭi**—hut: Vin IV 48
***kuḍuba**—measure of volume (4 *muṭṭhi* = 1 k.): Vism-a 361
***kuṇapa**—*also* ordure: Vism 259, 345
***kuṇḍa**—(*aggi-*) stove (?): Vism-a 37
***kuṇḍika**—(4-footed) water-pot: Vism 170
***kummāsa**—food made of wheat flour (PED gives "junket"): Khuddas 85; Vin IV 83; Vin-a 823

kulaputta—clansman {2 kinds: M-a I 180}

***kulumba**—foetus (= *gabbha* or *kula*: As-mṭ 76): Dhs-a 90-91

kusala—(1) skilful; (2) good; (3) (kammically) profitable, <wholesome> [def. Dhs-a 38-39, 62]

kusīta—idle, <lazy> {4 kinds: M-a III 358; 8 *kusīta-vatthu*: A IV 332}

kuhanā—scheming (to deceive) {3 *kuhunā-vatthu*: Nidd I 224} [def. Vibh 352]

***kūṭa**—*also* wild, savage: Vism 268; M-a II 82

***kūṭāgāra**—*also* (1) catafalque in which bier is carried to charnel ground: M-a IV 39; (2) palanquin in which a traveller is carried: Vism 390; M-a V 90

***kūpa**—pit, well, cesspit: Khuddas 167

***kūpaka-yaṭṭhi**—masthead, spar (?): Vism 657

***ketakī**—kind of plant: Khp-a 46

***keḷaṇā**—(from *keḷāyati*) tricking out (in finery), pranking: Vibh 351

***koccha**—*also* a brush: Kkh 80

***koṭika**—(*dvi-, catu-*) proposition in double, quadruple relation (log.): Vism 653; *ubhato-koṭika-pañhā*—dilemma, two-pronged question: M I 393

***koṭṭha**—flat (*koṭṭh-aṭṭhi*—"flat bone" = shoulder-blade, not "stomach-bone" (!) as in PED): Vism 254-55

***koṭṭhalika**—flattened: Vism 252

kodha—anger [def. Vibh 357]

***kosa**—measure of length (about 1 mile): Vism 127; Vism-a 123 (1 k. = 2000 *dhanu*)

***kriyā**—verb (gram.): Khp-a 17

kriyā—functional (consciousness or mind): Vism 456

***kriyā-visesa**—adjective (gram.)

KH

***khajjūrika**—kind of plant (the wild date-palm): Khp-a 49

khaṇa—moment {3 kinds: Vism-a 423}
***khaṇati**—*also* to consume (in exegesis of *sukha* & *dukkha*): Vism 145, 527; As-mṭ 92
***khaṇitti**—spade: M-a II 347
khanti—patience
***khanti**—*also* preference, liking; acquiescence in: M II 171ff., 218; Vism 434; Khp-a 19,134
khandha—aggregate {the 5 = *rūpa-, vedanā-, saññā-, saṅkhāra, viññāṇa-*; also the 5 = *sīla-, samādhi-, paññā-, vimutti-, vimuttiñāṇadassana-*}
khaya—exhaustion, destruction [def. Vism 293, 508; M-a I 63; Dhs-a 58]
khara—hard, solid
***kharapā**—raw, uncooked: Khuddas-a 85
***kharigata**—solidified: M I 185; Vibh 82
khāra—caustic {3 kinds: Vibh-a }
***khijjana**—excitement: Vism-a 450
***khinna**—fatigued, wearied, exhausted: Vism 145
***khipati**—*also* to sneeze: Vin II 140
***khīṇa**—(pp. *khīyati*) also critical, censorious: M III 230
khīṇa—(pp. *khayati*) exhausted, destroyed
khīṇāsava—one whose cankers are destroyed {2 kinds: M-a IV 70; *-bala*: D III 283; Paṭis II 173; A IV 224}
***khīṇeti**—(caus. *khayati*) to cause destruction of: Vism 508
***khudā**—hunger: M-a IV 187
khura-cakka—razor-wheel (a figure used for *atricchatā*) Vibh-a 471
***khurappa**—hoof tip: M I 429
***khulukhulukāraka**—making a splashing noise: M II 138 (see PED *Corrigenda*)
khetta—field {the 3: M-a IV 114}
***khyāta**—celebrated: Khp-a 101

G - GH

***gaṇḍa**—*also* cheek: Khp-a 46; Abh 262

***gaṇḍikā**—wooden gong: Khp-a 223, 251

***gaṇḍuppādaka**—*also* worm in the body: Vism 258

***gaṇḍūsa**—*also* medicinal oil (?): Khp-a 64

gaṇhāti—to seize, to apprehend, to assume

***gata-paccāgata**—(1) duty of going to and returning from the alms round with the meditation subject: M-a I 257; (2) kind of refuse-rag for robe-making: Vism 62

gati—destination (upon rebirth)

***gada**—poison: M-a II 107 (*see*: *agada* in PED)

***gadati**—to enunciate: Vism 203 (*see: gada* in PED)

gantha—(1) tie (the 4); (2) book [def. Vism 683;.Vibh 374]

gandha—odour

***gandhabba**—*also* being about to be born (= *tatr'ūpaka-satto*: M-a II 310; not "(demigod) said to preside over childbirth conception" as in PED, which is unfounded. Derivation most likely fr. root √*gam* and gerundive suffix = *gantabba*, with insertion of aspirant on analogy of *nekkhamma*: the meaning then is "one who has to go": M I 265; II 157)

***gandhayati**—to be smelt: Vism 481

***gamī (gamin)**—what is gone to: Khp-a 18

***gammati**—to be gone to (pass. of root √*gam*): Khp-a 170

***galavāṭaka**—nape of the neck (not in this sense in PED, but elsewhere base of the neck seems indicated): M-a II 58; Vism 249; Vibh-a 232

gahaṇa—apprehending, assuming

***gāmaṇḍala**—a village boy (= *gāma-dāraka*: M-a III 411): M II 155

gāvuta—measure of length, quarter-league (80 *usabha* =1 *gāvuta*; 4 *gāvuta* = 1 *yojana*)

gāha—apprehension, assumption (*atta-* assumption of a self) {3 kinds: M-a II 110}

***gāhita**—(*vippaṭikkula-*) treatment (?): Vibh 351

guṇa—(1) special quality, virtue; (2) thread, strand, cord; (3) layer [def. M-a I 55]

gocara—(1) pasture; (2) domain, resort {3 kinds: Vism 19}

***gocchaka**—block (set of dyads in Abhidhamma Mātikā): Dhs p. 2

gotta—lineage

gotrabhū—change-of-lineage (state of consciousness preceding jhāna or path)

***gonasa**—kind of snake ("scorpion snake"?): A-a

***gopa**—(fr. *gopeti*) guardian, herdsman; M II 180; Vism 166

ghaṭi-kāla—o'clock (*nava-ghaṭikāle—at nine o'clock)

ghaṭṭana—impinging, knocking together

***ghaṭṭha**—(pp. of *ghaṃsati*) pressed down: Khp-a 49

ghana—compact {4 kinds: *santati-, samūha-, kicca-, ārammaṇa-* : Vism-a 68}

ghana-vinibbhoga—resolution of what appears compact (into elements)

ghāna—nose

C - CH

cakkavāḷa—world-sphere, universe (one of many which make up a *lokadhātu*: see M-a to MN 115)

***cakkhati**—to relish (?) (in exegesis of *cakkhu*): Vism 481; As-mṭ 136

cakkhu—eye, eyesight {2 kinds: S-a (Ce.) II 1; 3 kinds: D III 219; 5 kinds: M-a III 407} [def. Dhs 596; Vism 444-45, 481]

cakkhusamphassaja—born of eye-contact

***caṅgavāra**—seive (= *khāraparissavana*: M-a II 128): M I 142

catuttha-jhāna—fourth jhāna {13 kinds: Vibh-a 372}

***catutthī**—dative case (gram.)

***caturassā (kathā)**—one of the 3 kinds of *kathā*; "four-square" discourse, in which, e.g., the bad herdsman and bad bhikkhu are compared and then the good herdsman and the good bhikkhu, all rounded off with a conclusion (e.g., MN 34): M-a II 258; cf. *nisinnavattika*

catusamuṭṭhāna—(*rūpa*) of fourfold origination (i.e., by *citta, kamma, utu* and *āhāra*)

***capala**—personally vain (*see: cāpalya*): M I 32; III 6; (not as in PED)

***caraṇa**—art, <painting or art exhibition>: S III 151; Dhs-a 64

caraṇa—conduct

***carasā**—prowling: M I 449

cariya, carita—conduct, temperament {3 kinds: Paṭis I 79; Vism 101-2; 6 kds: Vism 101; 14 kds: Vism 101} [def. Vism-a 197]

cāga—(1) generosity; <(2) giving up>

***cāpalya (cāpalla)**—personal vanity: M II.167; Vibh 351; Vism 106 (so explained in Vibh-a and M-a on refs. given; PED gives "fickleness," which is wrong)

***cāraka**—prison: Vism 479, 495

***cikicchā**—(desiderative of *kicchati,* to cure) wish to be cured: Vism 471

citta—cognizance, (manner of) consciousness, mind (loosely synonymous with *ceto, mano* and *viññāṇa*; technically *viññāṇa* considered with its affective colouring, and classified as such into 89 kinds in Dhs); the oblique inflexions of *ceto* & *citta* are used indiscriminately for *citta* in the suttas {2 kinds: Vibh-a 413; 4 kinds: Vibh 405; 7 kinds: Vibh 401} [def. Dhs 6; Dhs-a 63f., 112; M II 26; S II 94]

citta-ṭṭhiti—steadiness of consciousness

cittavīthi—cognitive series (in the occurrence of consciousness; in the 5 doors composed of 17 members, namely: 3 *bhavaṅga*, 1 *āvajjana*, 1 seeing, (or hearing, etc.), 1 *sampaṭicchana*, 1 *santīraṇa*, 1 *voṭṭhapana*, 7 *javana*, 2 *tadārammaṇa*; in the mind-door composed of 3 *bhavaṅga*, 1 adverting, 7 *javana*, 2 *tadārammaṇa*)

citta-saṅkhāra—mental determination, <mental formation> (i.e., *vedanā* and *saññā*)

citta-samuṭṭhāna—(*rūpa*) originated by consciousness, mind-originated

cittuppāda—arising of consciousness or mind [def. Vism 684]

***cira**—rag (?): M-a II 259

***cilīma**—*should read*: *vilīmaṃsa* (q.v.): M III 274

***cīna**—China

cīyati—to accumulate: D II 136; M I 338; no sutta ref. in PED

***cuṇṇiya**—fragmentary, short (-*pada*—short quotation): M-a II 167

cuti—death (lit. fall)

cuti-citta—death consciousness: Paṭṭh 324; Vism 460

***culli (cūḷī)**—head-rest (made of ring of twisted cloth [?]): Khp-a 50

cetanā—choice, <volition> {3 kinds: M-a V 67; 4 kinds: Vibh 405; 7 kinds: Vibh 401; 12, 13 and 24 kinds: Vism 530} [def. Dhs 5; Vism 463; Vism-a 21]

cetanā-kāya—body of choice, <class of volition> {the 6: S III 60}

cetasika—mental (adj.), mental concomitant (n.) {7 kinds: Vism 589; 52 kinds: Abhidh-s Pt.II 1}

cetiya—shrine [def. Khp-a 221-22; 3 kinds]

ceto—mind, "heart" (see also: *citta*)

cetopariya-ñāṇa—encompassing of mind (with mind)

cetovimutti—deliverance of mind, heart-deliverance (term principally for *samādhi* and *sammā samādhi*) {6 kinds: M I 296-98}

copana—stirring, motor activity: Dhs-a 92

***chaṭṭhī**—genitive case (gram.)

chanda—zeal, <desire> [def. Vibh 208; Vism-a 387]

chādeti—*also* to sustain (life), <to be agreeable to>: M I 275 (see also: *acchādeti*)

cheka—genuine: M I 509

J - JH

***jajjharikā**—a kind of plant: M-a II 407

***jaññā**—*also* ger. of *jānāti*: M III 187, 230

***jatuka**—bat, pipistrelle: Vism 107

***janaka**—*also* father, begetter: Vism 575; Khp-a 82

***janayati**—to produce, to generate: Khp-a 170

***jappeti**—(*mānaṃ jappeti*) to work up (conceit): Vibh 353

***jara**—fever: A V 110; Vism 350; Nidd I 17

jarā—ageing, old age {2 kinds: Vism 502; 3 kinds: Vism 449} [def. D II 305; Vism 502]

jarā-maraṇa—ageing and death

***jalukā**—leech: D-a I 117; Khp-a 72

***jallaka**—wetness: Vibh 32

javana—(1) speed; (2) impulsion (consciousness): Paṭis I 80; II 72; member of *citta-vīthi*, q.v. {3 kinds: Dhs-a 74; 7 kinds: Vism 459}

jāta—born, produced

jāti—birth [def. D II 305; Vism 498]

***jāti-bhūmī**—birthplace: M I 145

***jāti-loha**—kind of metal {7 kinds: M-ṭ I 73}

***jānituṃ**—<to confiscate> (inf. of *jahati*?): M-a III 353

***jāpeti**—(caus. of *jahati*) to confiscate: M II 122

jivhā—tongue

jīva—soul

jīvita—life [def. Dhs 19,635; Vism 447, 464]

jīvita-saṅkhāra—vital determination, <vital formation> {the 3: Paṭis II 738 & Paṭis-a}

***juṭṭha**—fostered: Vism 491

jhāna—jhāna, meditation {2 kinds: Vism-a 146; 4 & 5 kinds: Vism Ch. IV} [def. M I 276f.]

jhānaṅga—jhāna factor {the 5: M I 294; the 7: Vism 539}

Ñ

***ñatta**—*also* renown: M I 318

ñāṇa—knowledge (in general sense) {2 kinds: D III 274; 3 kds: D III 275; 4 kds: Vibh 328-29; 33 kds: M-a II 26; 73 kds: Paṭis I 1-3; 77 kds: M-a II 26}

ñāṇa-cakkhu—eye of knowledge {5 kinds: S-a II 1 (Ce.)}

ñāṇa-cariya—behaviour of knowledge {the 16: Paṭis I 99}

ñāṇa-vatthu—basis for knowledge {44: S II 56; 77: S II 59}

ñāta—known

ñāta-pariññā—full knowledge of the known (*see*: *pariññā*)

***ñāyati**—(pass. of *jānāti*) to be known: Vism-a 240

***ñeyya**—what can be known: Paṭis I 134

ṬH

-ṭhaka—that stands on, that remains as a fixture, that lasts; *tatraṭṭhaka*—that remains where it is: Vism 65; *pabbataṭṭhaka* that stands on the mountain: Vibh-a 519; *mattaṭṭhaka*—that lasts a while: M I 185

***ṭhāna**—(1) place; (2) possibility (*ṭhānaṭṭhāna*—the possible & impossible); (3) reason [def. Dhs-a 53]

***ṭhānantara**—official position, post: M-a I 57; II 121

ṭhiti—(1) presence (*uppāda, ṭhiti, bhaṅga*: 3 moments of arising, presence & dissolution); (2) station, standing-place (*viññāṇaṭṭhiti*—station or standing-place of consciousness); (3) steadiness, stability (*cittassa ṭhiti*—steadiness of consciousness = weak concentration); (4) stagnation, stationariness

T - TH

takka—rational thought

takkana—act of rational thinking, reasoning

takkara—(*taṃ* + *kara*) one who does that

***tacchati**—to pare, to plane: M I 31; III 183; Vism 254

tajja—appropriate, <corresponding>

***tajjā-paññatti**—verisimilar description (concept): Pp-a 174

***tajjārī**—measure of length (36 *aṇu* =1 t.; 36 t. = 1 *rathareṇu*): Vibh-a 343 (see PED *Corrigenda*)

taṇhā—craving {2 kinds: A-a ; 6 *taṇhā-kāya*: M I 51; 18 *taṇhā-vicarita*: Vibh 392, 396; 108 kinds: Vibh 400} [def. D II 308; Vibh 136, 365; Vism 528]

tatra-majjhattatā—specific neutrality

tathāgata—Perfect One [def. M-a I 45f.]

tadaṅga—substitution of opposites (function of insight in substituting, e.g., perception of impermanence for perception of permanence); <in a certain respect>

***tadārammaṇa**—(1) having that (aforesaid thing) as its object; (2) registration (consciousness, which has the same object as the *javana* that preceded it in the *citta-vīthi*): Vism 459-60; the object of that: Vism 328

***taddhita**—secondary derivative substantive (gram.)

***tanana**—range: Vism 481

***tapassitā**—asceticism: M I 77

***tappika**—tormenting (*a-*): M-a V 107

***tappurisa**—dependent determinative compound (gram.)

tamo—(1) gloom (*caturaṅga-tamo*: S-a I 170); (2) turbidity (in Sāṃkhya system: Vism-a)

***tammaya**—(*see atammayatā*) unaloof, <identified with> (*no ca tena tammayo*: I remain aloof from it, <I do not identify with it>): M I 319

***tarala**—unsteady, fickle: Vism-a

***taḷāka**—lake: Khp-a 157

tādibhāva—equipoise (= *upekkhā*: Vism-a 222)

***tāvatva**—just-so-much-ness: Vism 481

***ti-ṭṭhānika**—having three places: Vism-a 575

titthiya—(non-Buddhist) sectarian

***ti-pukkhala**—"the Threefold Lotus" (one of the five divisions of the Netti)

***tipu-cuṇṇa**—bath-powder (?): M-a IV 155

tiyaddhagata—included in the three periods of time

tiracchāna-kathā—pointless talk (*see*: *kathā*)

tiracchāna-yoni—the animal (lit. "horizontal") womb, animal birth

tiratana—the Triple Gem (Buddha, Dhamma, Saṅgha)

***tirokkha**—(opp. of *paccakkha*) hidden from the eyes, out of sight: M-a I 149

ti-lakkhaṇa—the three (general) characteristics (of impermanence, pain and not-self)

ti-santati-rūpa—form of triple continuity (= 3 decads present at the moment of rebirth-linking consciousness)

ti-samuṭṭhāna—(form) of triple origination (i.e., by *kamma*, *utu*, and *āhāra*, excluding *citta*)

tīraṇa—judgement, investigation

tuccha—empty, hollow

***tuvantuvaṃ**—reciprocal abuse, answering back: D II 59; M I 110; A IV 401; Vibh 390

***tūlikā**—kind of colour (?): M-a II 101

***tūlini**—silky: M I 128

tejo—fire, heat {5 kinds: Paṭis I 103} [def. M I 422; Vism 350, 351-53, 363, 365; Vibh 83; Vism-a 359]

***thaṇḍila-pīṭhaka**—<a kind of chair>: M-a II 385

thaddha—stiffened, stiff

***thāvariya**—landlord: Dhs-a 111

thīna-middha—lethargy and drowsiness [def. Vibh 253-54; Vism 469; M I 275-76]

***thullakumārī**—an old maid (= *mahallikā anuviddhakumārī*: Vibh-a 339): Vibh 247

thera-bhikkhu—bhikkhu of more than 10 years' seniority

theriya—belonging to the elders: Vism 711; Khp-a 78

D

***dakasītalika**—edible white water-lily: Vism 258

***dajja**—3rd. pers. sing. opt. of *dadāti* (= *dadeyya*): M II 261

***datti**—*also* saucer: M-a II 45

***dadhāti**—to put (in exegesis of *dhātu*): Vism-a 513

dabba—matter, material (= *drabya*)

***dabba-sambhāra**—*also* material framework (e.g., for a wattle and mud wall): Vibh-a 252

***darita**—worn away (by water): Vibh-a 367

***dava**—*also* fluid (= *drava*)

***davatā**—fluidity (= *dravatā*): Vism-a 459

dasaka—(1) decad (of *rūpa* = *aṭṭhaka* + 2 additional elements, i.e., *jīvita* in each case and any one of the following: eye, ear, nose, tongue, body, sex, heart-base); (2) decade {3 kinds: Vism 613; 10 kinds: Vism 616}

dassana—seeing, vision

***dātta**—sickle: Khp-a 50; Abh 448

dāna—giving, gift

***dāna**—gap: Vism 60

***dāmarika**—ruffian, thug, brigand: M-a I 34; IV 103

dāsa—bondsman {4 kinds: Vin-a 1000; Nidd I 11}

***dāsabya (dāsavya)**—bondsmanship: Vibh-a 487

***digu**—numerical determinative compound (gram.)

diṭṭha—seen

diṭṭhi—view, (right) view, (wrong) view [def. Dhs 20, 381; Vibh 104; Vism 509]

diṭṭhigata—recourse to views, field of views {6 kinds: Paṭis I 130;2 kinds: It 43}

diṭṭhiṭṭhāna—standpoint for views {8 kinds: Paṭis I 138}

diṭṭhi-nijjhāna-khanti—choice after pondering over (illustrating) views, <acceptance of a view as a result of reflection> (PED gives conflicting meanings under the various components)

diṭṭhippatta—one attained (to the noble path by predominance in) right view {6 kinds: M-a III 189}

diṭṭhi-samudaya—origin of view {2 kinds: M-a II 11}

dibba-cakkhu—divine eye

dibba-sotadhātu—divine ear element

divasa-vihāra—daytime abiding

dukkha—pain, painful, suffering, unease, unpleasure, unpleasantness, ill [def. D II 305-6; Dhs 416; Vibh 99, 100, 106; Vism 462, 499-500, 503]

dukkha-dukkha—intrinsic suffering (i.e., painful feeling)

dukkha-lakkhaṇa-kāraṇa—reason for the characteristic of suffering {4 kinds: M-a II 113}

duggati—bad or unhappy destination {2 kinds: M-a I 167}

duccarita—misbehaviour, misconduct

***duṭṭha**—(pp. *dussati*) corrupted by hate (used as verbal adj. for *dosa*)

***duṭṭhulla**—*also* inertia (glossed by *ālasiya*): M I 435; III 151, 159; irritability: Vism 151

***dunnigamana**—hard to get away from: M-a I 71

***dubbaca**—unamenable to verbal correction, difficult to speak to (never means ill-spoken); see PED under *su-*: M I 95

***dussata**—ill-remembered: M I 520

dussati—to corrupt with hate (*dosa;* used as a verb from *dosa*)

***dussantappīya**—hard to satisfy: M-a II 139

deva—god, mode of address to king [def. M-a I 33; Vibh-a 518]

desa—(1) place, location; (2) part: *eka desa-sarūp'ekasesa*—making one member of a whole represent any of the others (gram.): Vism 561-62, 565; (3) *desantaruppatti*—successive arisings in adjacent locations (in explanation of phenomenon of motion): Vism-a 452

desanā—teaching, showing {2 kinds: M-a I 137}

***desantaruppatti**—*see under*: *desa* (3)

doṇi—measure of volume (16 *nāḷi* = 1 *doṇi*)

domanassa—grief [def. D II 306; Dhs 417; Vism 461, 504]

dovacassatā—(n. fr. *dubbaca*) resistance to admonition [def. Vibh 359; Dhs-a 52]

***dosa**—humour (of the body): Vism 103

dosa—hate (n.) [def. Dhs 418; Vibh 362; Vism 470]

***dosa**—angry (adj.): Pāṭim, Vin Saṅghādisesa 8

***drabya**—matter, material (= *dabba*): Vism-a 753; M-ṭ II 91

***drava**—fluid (= *dava*): Vism 351; Vism-a 361

***dravatā**—fluidity (= *davatā*): Vism-a 459

dvāra—door; *pañca-*, the 5 doors (of the eye, ear, nose, tongue and body); *kamma-* , door of action (i.e., body, speech and mind); *mano-* , the mind-door {5 kinds: Vism 459; 9 kinds: Vism 346}

DH

***dhaññamāsa**—measure of length (7 *ūkā* = 1 dh.; 7 dh. = 1 *aṅgula*)

dhanu—(1) bow; (2) measure of length (2000 dh. = 1 *kosa*)

***dhamakaraṇa (dhammakaraṇa)**—filtering-cup: Nidd I 324; Vibh-a 481

dhamma—In general: ideas, dhamma (ger. of *dharati*—to bear, to remember—and of *dahati*—to put; lit. "what can be carried in the mind"). In particular: (1) dhamma, idea; (2) the Dhamma, <=the Buddha's Teaching> (the "True Idea"); (3) dhamma, state; (4) idea (as in 12th base), object of mind-consciousness. Loosely and inaccurately: thing, phenomenon. For commentarial definitions see: D-a I 99; Dhs-a 38; M-a I 17 {5 kinds: Dhs-a 95-96}

dhamma—inseparable from the idea of, subject to, having the nature of (vayadhamma—inseparable from the idea of fall, having the nature of fall)

dhammaṭṭhiti-ñāṇa—knowledge of relationship of ideas <or states>, knowledge of structure of ideas <or states> (term for dependent origination)

dhammatā—natural law, essentialness to the idea of

***dhammatā-rūpa**—natural form (i.e., stones, trees, etc.): Vism 625

dhamma-dhātu—(1) idea element, <element of mind-objects>; <(2) element of things: M I 396; S II 56> [def. Vibh 89; Dhs 69]

***dhammani**—rat-snake: Vism 358; S-a III 7

dhamma-nijjhāna-khanti—choice after pondering over the True Idea (Dhamma); <acceptance of the Dhamma as a result of reflection>

dhamma-vavaṭṭhāna—definition of ideas <or states> (opp. of *vicikicchā*) {9 kinds: Paṭis I 84}

dhammavicaya—investigation of ideas <or states> (of the True Idea, of dhammas, of the Dhamma)

dhammānusārin—one mature in the Dhamma

dhammāyatana—idea base, <base of mind-objects> [def. Dhs 66; Vibh 72]

***dhammin**—thing qualified (log.): Vism-a

***dhammuddhacca**—agitation about whether a state is of the noble path or not: Paṭis II 100; Vism 633

dhammūpanissaya—support for the Dhamma or True Idea {the 5: M-a II 89}

***dharaṇī**—the earth (*-talaṃ bhinditvā viya*): M-a III 350

dhātu—(1) element; (2) (bodily) humour [def. Vism 485]

***dhātu**—(1) verbal root (gram.); (2) (metal) ore: Vism 345; (*vaṇṇa-*) colour paint: Vism 172

***dhīyati**—to be borne (in exegesis of *dhātu*): Vism 485

dhutaṅga—ascetic practice (the 13)

***dhutta**—(*soṇḍikā-*) (brewer's) mixer, shaker: M I 228

***dhura-bhatta**—meal given in a principal house: Vism 66 (not as in PED)

dhuva—everlasting

***dhūnaka**—an instrument for carding cotton: Vism-a 844

N

nati—bent, bias

natthika-vāda—theory of nullity (in giving, etc.), <ethical nihilism>

nadī—river {the 5: Vism 416; Vism-a 412}

nandi—relish, relishing, <delight, delighting>

napuṃsaka-liṅga—neuter gender (gram.)

***namakkāra**—paying homage: M-a II 128

namati—to bend on to, to apply

naya—(1) method; (2) induction {5 kinds: Nett 2}

naya-vipassanā—inductive insight (= *kalāpa-sammasana*: Vism 606)

***nayana**—*also* act of leading, of inducing: Vism 481; Vibh-a 45

***nayana-nipāta**—glance with the eye: M-a I 14

***narati**—(in exegesis of *nara*, man): Vism-a 12

***narassika**—manly, masculine: M II 143

navaka—ennead (of form) = the *aṭṭhaka* + sound

nava-bhikkhu—bhikkhu with less than five years' seniority

***nahanā**—(fr. *nayhati*) tying: Vism 27

***nāganāsila-loha**—(= *vijāti-loha*) kind of metal: M-ṭ I 73

***nāgabalā**—kind of tree (Sinh. *domba*): Vism 261, 344

nāṭaka—dancer {3 kinds: Vism 399; Vism-a 394}

nānakkhaṇika—(kamma) acting from a different (earlier) moment of time

nānatta—difference, variety

nānā—different

nāma—(1) a name; (2) name, <mentality> (as the 3 aggregates: *vedanā, saññā,* and *saṅkhārā*); (3) noun (gram.) {4 kinds: Vism 209; Paṭis-a212} [def. Vibh 136; Vism 209-210, 528; Dhs-a 51]

nāma-kāya—the name-body, mental-body (term for the three mental aggregates excluding consciousness: *not* equivalent of *nāmarūpa* as stated in PED)

***nāma-nāma**—substantive (gram.)

nāma-paññatti—name-description (concept): Pp-a 171

nāma-rūpa—name-and-form, <mentality-materiality> (term for 4 of the 5 khandhas omitting consciousness as used in the suttas, but sometimes for all 5 aggregates as used in the Commentaries) [def. M I 53; Vibh 136; Vism 528]

nāmarūpa-vavatthāna—definition of name-and-form, <of mentality-materiality>

***nāma-visesa**—adjective (gram.)

***nāyati**—(= *ñāyati*: Vism-a 295) is known: Vism

***nāyare**—(3rd pers. pl. pres. middle *jānāti*) = *ñātanti*: Vism 236

***nārāyaṇa**—radiance, beam, flash: M-a II 26

***nāḷi**—*also* measure of volume (4 *kuḍuba* = 1 n.; 16 n. = 1 *doṇa*; also 1 *nāḷi* = 1 *pattha*)

nikanti—attachment, attraction

nikkha—coin (1 n. = 5 *suvaṇṇa*: M-a IV 152; 1 n. = 20 or 25 *suvaṇṇa*: M-ṭ III 321)

***nikkhepa**—*also* (1) *suttanikkhepa*—delivery of a sutta {4 kinds: *attajjhāsaya*—according to the speaker's inclination; *parajjhāsaya*—according to another's inclin.; *pucchāvasika*—as result of a question; *atthuppattika*—on account of a need arisen: M-a I 15; (2) placing (of a sutta) in a collection, position there: Khp-a 75, 89

***nigganṭhika**—not intricate: Vibh-a

***niggamana**—(*dun-*) with (difficult) exit: M-a I 71

***niggaha**—refutation: Kv 1

***niggahīta**—the consonant *ṃ* (= *anusvāra*)

***niggahīta**—refuted: Kv 2; M II 3

***niggaheti**—to rebuke: M-a II 307

***nigghāta**—mental depression: Vism 370

nicca—permanent

***niccakappaṃ**—(adv.) constantly: M III 266

***niccam-atāṇa**—permanently without refuge: Paṭis I 129

***niccoriyati**—to be sifted (gloss for *vaṭṭayamāna*): Vism-a

nicchaya—(adv.) certainly, exactly

niccharaṇa—utterance

nijjīva—soulless

nijjhatti—<persuasion>: M I 320 (*nijjhatti-bala*—power of persuasion: Paṭis II 176)

nijjhāna—illustrating, brooding, pondering, <contemplating>

nijjhāpeti—<to persuade>: Paṭis II 176; M I 320

***niṭumba**—spelling of *niṭamba* at Vibh-a 367

***niṭṭhura**—scorning: Vibh-a 493

***niṭṭhuriya**—scorn (so according to Vibh-a 493): Vibh 357

***niḍahati**—to burn: Vibh-a 101

***nideti**—to produce: M-a II 18

niddesa—(1) detailed exposition, demonstration, demonstrative; (2) name of 2 books in Tipiṭaka

***niddhāraṇa**—*also* deduction: Vism-a 354; emphasis: Vism-a ; withdrawal: Khp-a 224

nidhi—store {4 kinds: Khp-a 217}

nipāta—(1) dropping (*see*: *nayana-nipāta*); (2) particle (gram.)

***nippadesa**—comprehensive, inclusive (cf. *sappadesa*): Vism 514; Dhs-a ; Vibh-a 391

***nippapañca**—non-diversification: M I 65; A III 431; IV 229

***nippariphanda**—inactive: Vism 171

***nippariyāya**—*also* direct, literal, non-metaphorical (*nippariyāyena*—literally): M-a I 89 (see also: *pariyāya*)

***nippiṃsati**—to scrape off, to grind away: Vism 29; Vibh-a 485

***nippuñchati**—to wipe off: Vism 29; Vibh-a 485

***nippesikatā**—belittling (lit. "scraping off"): M III 75; Vism 29; Vibh 353 (not as in PED)

***nippeseti**—(caus. of *nippiṃsati*) to scrape off: Vism 29; Vibh-a 485

***nipphanna**—produced (term for certain kinds of *rūpa*)

***nibbacana**—verbal derivative (gram.): Vism 60, 494; M-a I 61, 105; Vibh-a 83-84

***nibbaṭṭita**—picked over: Vism 657 (*-kappāsa*)

nibbattati—is generated, is reborn

nibbatti—generating, rebirth, production

nibbāna—extinction (of *rāga, dosa, moha*); *nibbāna* = 3rd Noble Truth (2 *nibbāna-dhātu*: It 38) [def. It 38; S IV 251; Vism 293, 507f.; Vism-a 534-40; Vibh-a 51f.]

***nibbikappa**—"without thinking about," without planning

nibbidā—dispassion, revulsion

nibbindati—to become dispassionate towards (with loc.)

***nibbinna**—pp. of *nibbindati*: Vism-a 536

***nibbisa**—without poison: Vism 208, 401

nibbedha—penetration
nimitta—(1) sign; (2) for the sake of (encl.) {2 kinds: D III 213; Vism 125; 3 kinds: A I 256-57; Vism 125}
***nimmathita**—*also* produced: M II 130
***nimmada**—without vanity: M-a I 56
nimmāna—creation
nimmita—created
niyata—certain, invariable
niyati—fate
niyati-vāda—theory of determinism, fatalism
***niyanti-viññāṇa**—consciousness that leads to rebirth (= *saṃvattanika-viññāṇa*): M-a IV 66
***niyamita**—demonstrative pronoun (e.g., *so*) (gram.)
***niyāma**—certainty
***niyuñjana**—act of stimulating: Khp-a 132
***niyyātana**—*also* assigning: Vibh-a 12; setting going: Vism 449
niyyāna—outlet
niyyānika—giving an outlet, <emancipating>
***niruḍha**—spelling of *niruḷha*: Vibh-a 513
***niruttara**—(1) one without superior: Abhi-av 1; (2) one who cannot give a conclusive reply to a refutation
nirutti—language, expression
nirutti-patha—mode of language {3 kinds: S III 71}
***nirūpita**—differentiated (*anirūpitarūpena*—in undifferentiated form): Vism-a 190
***nirūpeti**—to wield power: M-ṭ II 264
nirodha—cessation {2 kinds: M-a II 299; Vism 508} [def. D II 310; S III 24; Vibh 103; Vism 506f.]
nirodha-samāpatti—cessation attainment (= *saññāvedayita-nirodha*): S II 151 (no sutta ref. in PED)
***nillekhana**—scraping: M-a II 228
***nillehaka**—licking: Vin Sekhiya 51-53

***nisinnavattika**—sutta in which e.g., the bad herdsman, bad bhikkhu, good h. and good bh. are each treated right to the conclusion before the next is started (as opposed to the *caturassā kathā*, q.v.): M-a II 258

***niseti**—to sharpen: Dhs-a 90

***nisevita**—well imprinted (?) (= *nighaṃsita*: M-a II 198): M I 178

nissajja-dosa—fault in sitting down {6 kinds: M-a I 110}

nissatta—no-creature, not a creature, not a being

nissaya—(1) support, physical support; (2) dependence (given by teacher to pupil) {2 kinds: Vism 12}

nissaraṇa—escape

***nissasati**—to be anxious (*see*: *vissasati* in PED): M-a IV 170

***nissita-vacana**—dependent locution (where e.g., name of cause is given to fruit): Vism 21; Vism-a 40

***nihaniṃ**—1st pers. sing. aor. *nidahati* (?): M II 82

nīvaraṇa—hindrance [def. M I 275-76; Vism 684]

***nīhaṭa**—faultless: M III 243

***nīharati**—*also* to fix: Vism 72

***nīhāra**—film (of oil): Khp-a 65

***nuhi (nuhī)**—kind of plant: Khp-a 46; Abh 587

nekkhamma—renunciation

***nemittika**—(a name) signifying an acquirement: Vism 209

***nemittikatā**—*also* hinting: M III 75; Vism 23; Vibh 352

P

***paṃsadhovaka**—earth-washer (?): Khp-a 30

***paka**—a drinker: Ud 91

pakaṭṭha—distant: Vism 216 (= *dūra*: Vism-a 227)

pakati—(1) nature; (2) normal, natural

***pakati**—Primordial Essence, Prakṛti: Vism 513, 518, 525; Vism-a 752

***pakāsa**—lighting up: Vism 535

pakāsana—explanation

pakāseti—to explain

pakkhandati—to enter into, to launch out into, to leap forth (in exegesis of *saddhā*)

pakkhandana—act of entering into, launching out into

***pakkhapāsa**—lath (of roof): Dhs-a 83 (*see* As-mṭ)

***pakkhepa**—assumption, <positing>(?): M-a I 244

paguṇa—proficient, familiar

paggaha—exertion [def. Dhs 56]

paccakkha—actual personal experience ("before one's eyes")

paccatta—for oneself

***paccatta-vacana**—nominative case (gram.)

***paccanīkatā**—opposition: M I 402

***paccanubhoti**—to experience, to have access to, to exploit, to be coessential with, to exploit for one's being (existence): M I 295; Khp-a 209 (*paccanubhavantā*)

***paccapādi**—3rd. pers. sing. aor. of *paṭipajjati*: M III 270

***paccabyatha (= paṭividdhatha)**—Vin I 40; Vin-a 975 (Ee & Be: *paccabyattha*); Ap-a 231, Th-a III 95, Vjb 416

paccaya—(ger. of *paṭi* + *eti* used as noun) (1) condition (for what is conditionally arisen) (the 24: Paṭṭh 1); (2) requisite, necessary condition for the bhikkhu life (the 4)

paccayatā—conditionality

paccaya-pariggaha—discernment of conditionality (preparation for insight)

paccaya-samuppanna—conditionally arisen

paccayākāra—structure of conditionality (term for dependent origination)

paccavekkhaṇa—reviewing {2 kinds: Vism 676; 5 kinds: Vism 676; 10 kinds: M-a I 268; 19 kinds: Vism 676}

***paccāhāra**—excuse: S-a I 306

***paccuddharati**—formally to renounce ownership of a robe: Vin II 151

paccupakāra—recompense: M-a V 70

paccupaṭṭhāna—manifestation

paccuppanna—the present (time), present, presently arisen {3 -*addhā*: Vibh-a 7}

***pacchābhattika**—one who, while eating food given only before noon, refuses any extra food after he has accepted his meal; after-food refuser (a practiser of one of the 13 *dhutaṅga*)

pajānāti—to understand

pañcamī—ablative case (gram.)

pañca-viññāṇāni—the five consciousnesses (i.e., eye, ear, nose, tongue, and body consciousness)

***pañjara**—frame (not quite in this sense in PED): Vism 255; Vibh-a 238

paññatti—(1) description (concept) (see Pp-a); <(2) prescription (of training rule)>

paññā—understanding, <wisdom> (i.e., in one who has reached the path or is practising insight for it, or else "native wit") {3 kinds: Vibh 324-25; 4 kinds: Vibh 329-30} [def. S V 197; Dhs 16; Vibh 350; Vism 436f.; M-a IV 83f.]

paññāpīyati—to be caused to be described, to be made manifest

paññāpeti—(1) to describe; (2) to lay out (robe), to prepare (a seat); <(3) to promulgate, to lay down (a training rule)>

paññāyati—to be understood, <to be discerned, to be manifested>

paññā-vimutta—liberated by understanding <or wisdom> {5 kinds: M-a III 188}

pañha—question (see also: *ovaṭṭikasāra-pañha, ānīta-pañha*) {4-*vyākaraṇa*: D III 229}

***paṭatantuka**—kind of worm in the body: Vism 258

***paṭapaṭeti**—to crackle: Vibh-a 4; Vism 626

*__paṭalita__—played (of musical instrument): Khp-a 172

*__paṭikamma__—rejoinder after inconclusive refutation (log.): Kv 2

*__paṭikaroti__—*also* to obey: M III 133

*__paṭikāra__—<?> M-ṭ II 260

*__paṭikkamana__—refectory: Vism 66; Sn-a 53

paṭikkūla—repulsive

paṭigha—(1) resistance (resentment) [def. Vibh 167]; <(2) sensory impingement [def. Vism 329]>

paṭicca—(ger. of *paṭi* + *eti*) having depended, due to, dependent on

*__paṭicca__—(as last but decl. adj.) ought to be arrived at: Vism 521; Vibh-a 465

paṭicca-samuppanna—dependently arisen

paṭicca-samuppāda—dependent origination [def. D II 55f.; M I 46f., 259f.; S II 1f.; A I 177; Vibh 135f.; Vism Chs. XVII and XIX]

*__paṭijānāti__—(1) to claim: M I 69; (2) to make a logical proposition (log.): Kv 2

paṭiññā—claim

*__paṭiññā__—proposition, first member of syllogism (log.): Vism 532; Kv 2; Vism-a

paṭiniddesa—redescription

*__paṭiniyata__—certain, definite: Vism-a

*__paṭiniyyāteti__—to discharge (an obligation): M-a II 317

paṭinissagga—relinquishment

paṭinissajjati—to relinquish

paṭipatti—way, progress, practice

*__paṭipatti__—theory: Vism 468, 471, 528, 583; Vibh-a 137

paṭipadā—way; *also* name for certain suttas (see S-a III 291; M-a I 92; III 6; Vism 93) {3 kinds: A I 295; 4 kinds: D III 228} [def. Vibh 104, 106, 331; Vism 509f.; Vism-a 92]

*__paṭipadāna__—maintaining (on course); producing: Vism 128

paṭipannaka—one entered on the way {4 kinds: M-a II 137}

***paṭipassanā**—looking back: Vism 278

***paṭipāṭiyamāna**—following successively in order: Vism 245

***paṭipāda**—placing end to end: Vibh-a 117

paṭipuggala—person who is the equal of another person

***paṭipuggalika**—*see*: *pāṭipuggalika*

paṭibaddha—(1) bound up with; (2) ready to (his adverting) (*āvajjana-*): Paṭis I 172

paṭibhāga—counterpart

paṭibhāga-nimitta—counterpart-sign

paṭibhāṇa—perspicuity (intelligence) (4th of the 4 *paṭisambhidā*)

***paṭibhāṇeyyaka**—*also* one who arouses (others') intelligence: A I 25 (see A-a)

***paṭivatti**—performance (?), but better reading is *paṭipatti*: Khp-a 240

***paṭivānarūpa**—displeased: M II 244

paṭivijjhati—to penetrate, to pierce, to prick

***paṭivipassanā**—insight into past insight (as impermanent, etc.): Vibh-a 423

paṭivibhatti—sharing {2 kinds: D-a 33}

***paṭiveti**—to vanish: Vism 630; M III 25

paṭivedha—penetration, piercing

paṭisaṃvedeti—to experience

paṭisaṅkhā—having reflected, reflexion

***paṭisaṅkhārāpati**—to fortify: M III 7

paṭisandhi—(1) link: M III 230 (PED gives no sutta ref.); (2) rebirth-linking, rebirth-linking consciousness: Paṭis I 11; II 72; Paṭṭh 74 (not "metempsychosis" as in PED) [def. Vism 457, 545]

paṭisambhidā—discrimination {the 4: *attha-* = d. of meanings; *dhamma-* = d. of ideas <or states>; *nirutti-* = d. of language; *paṭibhāṇa-* = d. of perspicuity (in expression and knowledge)} {3 kinds: Vibh 297} [def. Vibh 293; Vism 440]

***paṭisiddha**—excluded, denied (log.): Vibh-a 164, 339; Vism 555; M-a I 85; IV 123
***paṭisedha**—exclusion, negation (log., gram.)
***paṭissaya**—gloss for *vihāra*: Vism-a 63
***paṭihaññati**—to resist, resent (as verb for *paṭigha*): Vism 320; Dhs-a 72
***paṭihāra**—(1) (*vāda-*) defense (M II 220) (2) escort: M-a IV 133
***paṭihita (paṇihita?)**—drawn on: A III 306
***paṭṭhita**—gone out (= *nikkhanta*: M-a): M I 79
***paṭhama-purisa**—3rd person (gram.)
***paṭhamī**—nominative case (gram.)
paṭhavī—earth {4 kinds: M-a I 25} [def. M I 421; Vibh 82; Vism 349, 351-53, 363, 365; Vism-a 359]
***paṇati**—to bargain price up: M-a III 194
***paṇāli**—slit: M-a IV 215 (= *chidda*: M-ṭ)
paṇidhi—disposition, desire
paṇihita—desired, to which one is disposed
paṇīta—sublime, superior, the (more) sublime [def. Vism-a 92]
***paṇopana-vidhā**—bargaining, haggling: M I 480
***paṇḍati**—to pick one's way, to be wise (exegesis of *paṇḍita*): Khp-a 124
paṇḍita—wise (3 *-paññatta*: A I 151; 3 *-lakkhaṇa*: A I 102)
patati—to fall
***patati**—to gather; to wander for: Vism 60
***pati**—*also* concerning, about (prep.): Vism-a to Vism 507
***pati**—3rd. pers. sing. aor. of *patati*
patiṭṭhāpana—founding: Paṭis II
***patīyamāna**—being gone back to: Vism 521
***pattaṅga**—kind of plant: Vism 173
pattha—measure of volume (1 p. = 1 *nāḷi*; also 4 p. = 1 *āḷhaka*)
***patthaṭa**—(*a-*) (un-) sought-after: Vibh-a 467

patthanā—aspiration {2 kinds: M-a I 41}

***patthanīyatā**—famousness, state of being sought after: Vism 118

patha—way, mode, course, track

***pathati**—to keep on the track, to carry on (*apathamāna*
not carrying on): Vibh-a

pada—(1) state; (2) word; (3) foot (in verse); (4) part of speech (gram.); [4 *padāni*, 4 parts of speech: *nāma* (nouns, adjs., pronouns); *ākhyāta* (verbs); *nipāta* (particles: adv., prep., interjections, etc.); *upasagga* (prefixes)]

***padaccheda**—elision of a word (gram.)

***padalopa**—elision of a word (gram.)

***padasiddhi**—establishment (derivation) of word (gram.)

padahati—to control, to endeavour

padahana—act of controlling, of endeavouring

***padumaka**—kind of wood: M II 152

***padose**—in the evening, in the dark: Khp-a 151 (cf. *dosā* in PED)

padhāna—endeavour, control {2 kinds: A I 49; *see samma-*} [def. Vism 679]

***padhāna**—the Basic Principle (Sāṃkhya system): Vism 511; Vism-a

***padhāvin**—traveller: M II 98 (the proper spelling is *pathāvin* as at M I 333 and Vin III 108 (see Vin-a 859 and M-a II 417); meaning given under *padhāvin* in PED should be deleted)

papañca—(1) obstacle, delay: Vism 125; (2) diffuseness: M-a I; (3) diversification (by craving, conceit and wrong views according to Commentary): M I 109 (not obsession as given in PED) {3 kinds: M-a I 157, 183}

papañceti—to diversify (as function of craving, conceit and wrong view, according to Commentary)

***pabbaka**—(*vīṇā-*) body (of lute) (?): Vibh-a

pabbata—rock, mountain ("larger than an elephant": Vibh-a 366) {5 kinds: M-a III 135}

***pabbanīya**—(lunar) quarter-day: Khp-a 114

***pabbāhati**— = *pabāhati*

***pabbhāra**—*also* overhang of rock (under which a cave dwelling can be made: Vism 75; Vism-a 107)

***pabyāharati**—(*pa* + *vi* + *ā* + *harati*) to announce, to utter: M-a I 152

pabhava—providing with being (production) (*ime … cattāro āhārā … kimpabhavā? … ime … taṇhāpabhavā*—What provides these four kinds of nutriment with being? Craving provides them with their being); *also* giving being, giving existence (function of a *paccaya*): M I 67, 261

***pabhavati**—to give being, to give existence (function of a *paccaya*): M I 329

pabhavana—act of providing with being (act of producing)

***pabhavika**—that which provides being (that which produces): M II 106 (*piya-pabhavika*—which endears itself)

pabhassara—transparent, limpid

pabhā—radiance {4 kinds: A II 139}

***pabhāvanā**—causing provision with being (production): Paṭis I 185

***pabhivatta**—selected: M II 51

***-pabhuti**—(encl.) also, and so on, et cetera (= *-ādi*): Vism 233, 258

pabheda—class, category

pamāda—negligence

***pamukha**—a forecourt: Vism 120; a verandah: Vism 342, 409; M-a III 351 (= *ālinda*): Vism-a 391

payoga—(1) means; (2) instrumentality: Khp-a 29, 39; M-a I 6; (3) addition: Khp-a 19 (*a-*)

payojana—purpose

***payojayitar**—one who takes a purpose upon oneself: M-a IV 195

***paradavutta**—(*para* + *da* + *vutta*) dependent on others' gifts (not as in PED; *see* M-a III 167): M I 450

***parapiṭṭhimaṃsikatā**—stabbing others in the back, "backbiting": Vibh 353

***paramāṇu**—smallest measure of length (hypothetical: 36 p. = 1 *aṇu*): Vibh-a 343; Vism-a 361

paramattha—(1) the supreme goal (Paṭis I 180; II 184); (2) the ultimate sense (as opposed to *vohāra* and *sammuti*: this last meaning only used apparently in the Commentaries): M-a I 138

***parassapada**—active voice (of verb) (gram.)

***parācarayoga**—term for faulty construction in a sentence (example given: *appatvā nadiṃ pabbato, atikkamma pabbataṃ nadī*): Vism-a 520 (gram.)

parābhava—ruin

parāmaṭṭha—misapprehended (i.e., *sīla* of which more is expected than it is capable of providing, as e.g., *go-sīla*, or *sīla* in a *puthujjana* who has no *sammā diṭṭhi*): Paṭis I 42

parāmāsa—misapprehension (adherence); *sīlabbata-parāmāsa*—misapprehension of virtue and duty <or of rules and observances, rites and rituals> [def. Vibh 365; Vism 684]

parikathā—roundabout talk

***parikappa**—abstract conjecture: Vism-a 110

***parikappanatā**—conjecturing: Vism 102

parikamma—preliminary work

parikkamana—avoiding, by-passing: M I 43

***parikkilesa**—defilement: Khp-a 16; M-ṭ II 46

***parikkhaṇati**—to dig in: Vibh-a 476

***parikkhata**—*also* presented, available: Vism 463

parikkhāra—(1) equipment; (2) requisite or equipment for a bhikkhu (the 4, etc.)

***parikkhepa**—circumference: M-a IV 220

pariggaṇhāti—to grasp, to embrace, to discern, to appropriate as a chattel (*pariggaha*)

pariggaha—(1) inclusion; (2) embracing (*attha* of *sammā vācā*); (3) chattel; (4) reinforcement; (5) discerning (stage in insight)

paricita—consolidated, <familiarized>

pariccāga—giving up

pariccheda—(1) a chapter (of a book), a division; (2) delimitation

***pariccheda-rūpa**—delimiting-form (i.e., space): Vism 448, 451

parijānāti—to fully know (with the 3 kinds of *pariññā*)

pariññā—full knowledge {3 kinds: *ñāta-pariññā* f.k. of the known (q.v.), *tīraṇa-pariññā* f.k. as judgement, *pahāna-pariññā* f.k. as abandoning: Vism 606} [def. Vism 606, 692; M-a I 29]

pariṇāma—change

paritassati—to have anguish, <to be agitated>

paritassanā—anguish, <agitation> {2 kinds: *bhaya*—due to fear, and *taṇhā*—due to craving: M-a III 390}

paritta—(1) small; (2) limited (term for the sensual-desire sphere); (3) protection (term for certain suttas recited for that purpose) [def. Vism-a 92]

parittatā—limitedness {2 kinds: Nidd I 43,117}

parideva—lamentation

***parinijjhāpana**—brooding, or burning up (with sorrow): Vism 503

***parinipphanna**—*also* positively-produced (term for *rūpa-rūpa*; cf. *nipphanna*): Vibh-mṭ 23

parinibbāna—attainment of extinction (either by full enlightenment (*sa-upādisesa-nibbāna*) or by the ending of the arahant's life-term (*anupādisesa-nibbāna*): It 38

parinibbāyin—one attaining extinction {5 kinds: A V 120}

paripācana—maturing (definition of *tejo-dhātu*: Vism 351)

***paripphandana**—*also* interference, activity: Vism 142, 465

***paribyākulatā**—perplexedness: Vism 102

***paribhaṭa**—(pp. *paribhaṭati*) nursed, carried about: Vism 28; Vibh-a 338

***paribhaṭati**—to nurse, to carry about (in exegesis of *paribhaṭyatā*): Vism 28; Vibh-a 338

***paribhaṇḍa**—(1) repairing: M-a I 291; IV 157; Vism 706; (2) stone or earth bench on verandah or at back of house: Khuddas 74

paribhuñjati—to use

paribhoga—(1) use; (2) utility

pariyatti—(1) mastery; (2) scripture {3 kinds: M-a II 107}

pariyādāna—(1) invasion, seizure {2 kinds: M-a II 61}; <(2) exhaustion>

pariyāpanna—(1) included; (2) included <within the world> (term for all *lokiyadhammā* as opposed to *lokuttaradhammā*)

pariyāya—(1) metaphor, figure of speech; (2) manner, way, method; (3) presentation, discourse [def. M-a I 18, 89]; (4) *pariyāya-vacana*—paraphrase: Khp-a 16

***pariyāhanana**—threshing, striking on: Vism 142

pariyuṭṭhāna—obsession {7 kinds: Vibh 383}

pariyogāhana—fathoming

pariyodāta—bright

pariyodāna—terminating

***pariyonahana**—covering, envelope: Vism 257

pariyosāna—end

***pariyosāna**—intensity (*pari* + *ava* + *sāreti* [?]): Vism 185

pariḷāha—fever (*kilesa-pariḷāha* fever of defilement)

***parivattaka**—*also* with turn-over (*see*: *anuparivattana*): Dhs-a 61

***parivattana**—*also* (1) turn-over (*see*: *anuparivattana*); (2) converting: Kkh 73

pariveṇa—*also* surroundings of a building, surrounding walk: Vism 152, 342

***parisaṇṭhita**—quiet (*aparisaṇṭhita*: turbulent): Vism 194

parisuddha—pure (*tikoṭi-* : M-a III 46)

***parissavati**—to flow away (= *vissavati*: Vism-a 361): Vism 365

***pariharitabba**—*also* to be avoided: Vism 475

parihāniya—detriment (6 *-dhamma*: Vibh 381)

***parihāra**—explanation, exegesis: Vism 543; M-a IV 141; implication: Vism-a 158

***parokkhā**—perfect tense (gram.)

***palala (phalla)**—(gloss for *tilapiṭṭha*): Vism-a 85

palāsa—domineering [def. M-a I 169]

***palāsati**—to domineer: Vibh-a 492

***palibuddha**—*also* stuck together: Vism 259

palibodha—impediment [def. Vism-a 97; M-a I 27; Khp-a 38]

***paluṭṭha**—scalded: Ud 22 (= *jhāmaya-paccaṅga*: Ud-a)

***pavaṭṭikā (paṭṭika, pavaḍḍhikā)**—piece of jewelry: M III 243

pavatta—occurred, occurrence (*see pavatti*)

pavatti—(1) occurrence: Vism 471; (2) course of an individual existence (excluding *paṭisandhi* and *cuti*): Vism 546

***pavana**—draught (of air): Vism 345, 500

***pavara**—upper (*kadaliṅga-pavara-paccattharaṇa*): M I 76

***pavāyita**—(*su*-) with the warp well stretched (in weaving of cloth): Vin III 259

***pavāraṇa-saṅgaha**—postponement of Pavāraṇa ceremony: M-a IV 138

pavicaya—investigation

paviveka—seclusion {3 kinds: M-a II 143}

***pavutta**—fallen (= *patita*: M-a IV 53): M II 254

pasaṅga—(see *atippasaṅga*) scope

***pasaṭa**—*also* relaxed: M-a I 280

***pasahati**—*also* to endure: Vism 501

pasāda—(1) clearness; (2) sensitivity (of *rūpa* = the 5 senses); (3) confidence [def. Vibh 170]

pasādana—confidence (the clearing of doubt in the mind by the act of faith = *saddhā*)

pasīdati—(1) to subside (e.g., cloudiness in water); (2) to acquire confidence

passaddhi—tranquillity

***pahaṃ (or pabhaṃ)**—most likely a contracted form of ppr. of *pahoti* (*pabhavati*): M I 329; D I 223 (where spoken by the Buddha, *not* by Baka Brahmā, see Be.); *sabbato-pahaṃ* (or -*pabhaṃ*) should probably resolve into *sabbato apahaṃ* and so refer to the *sabbato nāpahosiṃ* (so read with Be.) instead of the Ee *nāhosiṃ* 3 lines above in MN Sutta 49; derivation from root √*bhū* suggested in M-a

***pahāna**—abandoning, abandonment {3 kinds: Vism 693; 4 kinds: M-a I 71; Dhs-a 351; 6 kinds: M-a II 67}

***pahān'ekaṭṭha**—*see*: *ekaṭṭha*

***pahāya**—(ger. of *pahoti*)

pahitatta—(pp. *padahati* or (according to Comy.) of *pahiṇāti* + *attā*) self-controlled, self-exerted, <resolute>

pahīna—abandoned

***paheyya**—abandonable: Vism 514

pākata—evident, obvious

***pāga**—prior (-*bhāva*—immediately preceding state)

pāguññatā—proficiency (of *citta* and *kāya*)

***pāṭipuggalika**—belonging to an individual person (-*dāna* —gift to an individual person): M III 254; Dhs-a 46

***pāṭibhoga**—agent, intermediary, proxy (not quite as in PED): Vism 55-56

pāṭimokkha—the Rule of the Community {2 kinds: Ud-a 298}

pāṭihāriya—wonder, marvel {3 kinds: A I 170}

pāṇati—to breathe: Khp-a 241

pāṇātipāta—killing breathing things, <taking life>

***pāṇika**—*also* a trowel: Vism 124

***pāṇupeta**—*also* as long as breath (i.e., life) lasts: M I 24

***pātabyatā**—drinkability (fr. root √*pā, pivati*; not as in PED): M I 305

***pāda**—*also* part of a building: Dhs-a 107

***pāda**—*also* piece of money (5 or 2 *māsaka* = 1 p.; 4 p. = 1 *kahāpaṇa*)

***pādapīṭhika**—part of shrine: M-a III 246 (= Vibh-a 293, Dhs-a 72)

***pādānatā**—Khuddas 7

***pāduddhāra**—footstep, lifting of the foot: M-a I 260; Vism 202

***pāpaka**—(fr. *pāpuṇāti*) what reaches, causes to reach: Vism 437, 508

pāpaka—bad (= *pāpa*)

***pāpana**—(fr. *pāpuṇāti*) (1) reaching: Vism 508; Paṭis II 116; (2) the consequent (log.)

***pāpana**—(fr. *pāpa*) denigration: Vism 29, 353

pāpicchatā—evilness of wishes [def. Vibh 351]

***pāpiṭṭha**—bad: A I 148

pāmojja-mūlaka-dhamma—idea <state> that is a root of gladness {9 kinds: Paṭis I 85}

pāramī—perfection {10 kinds: M-a I 45; II 2; III 22; 30 kinds: Vism-a 181}

***pārāvata**—pigeon (spelling for *pārāpata*): Vism 342

***pārisesa**—limitation (*parisesena*—in a limited sense): As-mṭ 28-29

***pārihāriya**—special: Vism 98

pāḷi—text

***pāḷi**—(*vāpi-*) causeway, embankment: Vibh-a 446

pāḷi-muttaka—(method) not included in the texts

***pāvā**— = *pavadati*: Sn 782

***pāvāra**—*also* cloth: Vism 258

pāsaṇḍa—sect (96: M-a II 12)

***pāsati**—to throw: A-a

***pāsādanīya**—inspiring confidence, pleasing: M II 118; Ud 58

***piṇḍa**—stalk (of a toadstool): Vism 260

piṇḍapāta—almsfood {16 kinds: and 15 *piṇḍapātakhetta*: A-a }

***piṇḍika**—calf of the leg: Vism 252, 343

***pitar, cūḷa**—uncle: M-a II 61

***pittala**—kind of metal alloy <brass?>: M-ṭ I 43

***pidhānī**—lid: Vism 346

***pisati (piṃsati)**—*also* to beat, to pound (*uraṃ pisati*—he beats his breast): Vibh-a

***pisāca-loha**—kind of metal (not necessarily copper): Vibh-a 63 {8 kinds: M-ṭ I 73}

pisuṇa—malicious, <slanderous> (of speech)

***pīṇana**—act of refreshing: M II 188; Vism 146

pīti—happiness, <rapture, zest, joy> {3 kinds: S IV 235; 5 kinds: Vism 143} [def. Dhs 9; Vism 143]

pīneti**— = ***piṇeti—to refresh: Vism 143 (= M-a I 84)

***pīyataṃ**—(imp. of *pivati*?): M II 186

***puṃs**—masculine gender (gram.)

puggala—person {2 kinds: A I 76, etc.; 3 kinds: A I 107, etc.; Nett 7, etc.; 7 kinds: D III 253, etc.; 8 kinds: D III 255, etc.; 10 kinds: A V 23}

pucchā—questions {2 kinds: M-a II 328; 5 kinds: M-a II 334-35}

***pucchāvasika**—*see under*: *nikkhepa*

puñña—merit {3 kinds: Vibh 325}; *puññakiriyavatthu*—ground for making merit {3 kinds: It 51; 5 kinds: M II 205; 10 kinds: M-a I 132}

puññābhisanda—outcome of merit {4 kinds: A II 54}

***puttaka**—roller, rolling pin (gloss of *nisadapoṭa*): Vism-a 250

putta-maṃsa—child's flesh (allusion to S II 98f.; not as conjectured in PED): Vism 32; M-a I 16

puthujjana—ordinary man, <worldling> (i.e., who has not reached the path) {2 kinds: M-a I 20}

***puthuvacana**—plural (gram.)
***pupphaka**—balloon, swelling: Vism 258
***pupphula**—spelling of *bubbula* in Burmese texts
pubbakicca—preparatory task
pubbanimitta—portent {5 of deities' death: M-a IV 170}
***pubbenivāsānussati**—recollection of former life: M I 22
purakkhata—(encl.) preceded by, led by: Sn 199; M-a I 210
***purāṇa**—(*-taṇḍula*) *also* selected (rice): M-a I 294
***purindada**—First Giver (epithet of the Buddha): M I 386; see M-a III 98. PED seems to have gone astray
purisa—man, male (3 *purisa-sadassa*: A I 289; 7 *purisassa bhariyā*: A IV 92; 7 *purisa-gati*: A IV 70; (*purisa-mala*: Vibh 389) [def. Vism-a 12]
***purisa**—person (gram.)
***purisa**—World Soul (in Sāṃkhya system), *puruṣa*: Vism 518; Vism-a 752
***purekkhāra**—objective: Khp-a 40
pulliṅga—masculine gender (gram.)
***pekkha**—*also* stage show: D I 16
***pekkhatar**—seer, looker: Paṭis II 194
peta—(1) ghost; (2) departed one
pettivisaya—realm of ghosts
***pellana (phellana)**—pushing, propelling: Vism-a 270, 362; M-ṭ I 83
***pesika**—scraper: Vism 29
***poṭṭhalika**—*see*: *koṭṭhalika*
***pothetvā**—(ger.) having pressed: M-a V 67
***porisa**—*also* measure of height (foot to extent of fingertips extended above height)

PH

pharaṇa—act of extending, pervasion, intentness upon (= *ārammaṇa-karaṇa*)

pharati—to extend to, to pervade, to be intent upon

pharusa—harsh

phala—(1) fruit; (2) fruit of a reason {2 kinds: M I 62; 4 kinds: D III 227; 7 kinds: S V 314}; (3) fruition (of the noble path) (4 -*citta*: Vism 459)

***phalakasata**—target: Vism 674

phassa—contact, touch {4 kinds: Vibh 405; 6 kinds: M I 52; 10, 22, and 32 kinds: Vism 565} [def. M I 52; Dhs 2; Vibh 136; Vism 463, 528, 565]

phassa-kāya—body of contact (i.e., eye-contact, etc.) {6 kinds: M III 216}

phassati—to be touched, to contact

phassa-dvāra—door of contact {6 kinds: Dhs-a 95}

phassana—being touched, being contacted

phassa-pañcaka, phassa-pañcamaka—contact-pentad (in sutta forms: M I 53; III 25; in commentarial form: M-a I 249; Nett)

phassāyatana—base for contact {6 kinds: A II 161}

***phālaka**—a vessel: Khuddas 2

***phāsu**—comfortable: D II 99; Vism 118

phāsu-vihāra—comfortable abiding {5 kinds: A III 119}

***phudhamanaka**—branch of medicine: Vibh-a 410

***phullāpeti**—to blossom: M-a II 336

phusati—to touch

phusana—touching

phusīyati—to be touched

***phellana**—spelling of *pellana* (q.v.)

phoṭṭhabba—tangible (i.e., object of *kāyāyatana*) {3 kinds: as 3 of 4 *mahābhūta*: Vism 483} [def. Dhs 647]

B

***bajjhati**—(pass. *bandhati*) *also* to be responsible (for action: *kammunā bajjhati*): M-a I 200; Dhs-a 99; Khp-a 29

***baddha**—(1) imprisoned: M I 275; (2) responsible (for action: *kammunā baddho*): Khp-a 29

***bandha**—(1) imprisonment: M I 115; (2) responsibility (for action: *kammabandho*): Khp-a 29

***bandhati**—*also* to set up; *khandhāvaraṃ bandhati*—to halt a caravan: M-a V 44; *issaṃ bandhati*—to nurse envy: M III 204; *khandhāvaraṃ bandhitvā*—having made an encampment; *āghātaṃ bandhati*—to nurse a grievance: M-a III 24

***bandhana**—imprisonment: M I 275

bala—power [def. Vism 679]

balivadda—yoke ox {4 kinds: A II 108}

***balīpurisa**—conscripted man: Dhs-a 111

bavh-—compound form of *bahu* (e.g., *bavhatthena*)

bavhābādha—having much affliction {3 kinds: M-a III 358}

***bahala**—intense: M-a I 79

bahiddhā—(adv.) externally

***bahubbīhi**—relative compound (gram.)

bahulīkaroti—to cultivate, to make much of

bahuvacana—plural (gram.)

bahussuta—who has learnt much {2 and 4 kinds: D-a 530}

bāla—(1) child; (2) fool; (3) *-lakkhaṇa*: A I 102

***bālatta**—dotage: Vism 502

***bālavasanta**—name for month of Citta (approx. April): Khp-a 192

***bāliso**—(adv.) as a fool (?): M-a I 39

bāhira—(adj.) external

bāhiraka—(1) one outside the Buddha's Dispensation; (2) outward: M-a II 128

***bāhulika**—one who indulges in luxury: M I 171

***bindava**—spot (?): M-ṭ II

***bissanu**—Viṣṇu

buddha—enlightened; the Buddha, the Enlightened One {2 kinds: A I 77} [def. Vism 198f].

buddha-kicca—Enlightened One's function {5 kinds: S-a I 243}

buddha-kkhetta—Buddha's field {3 kinds: Vism 414}

buddha-guṇa—Enlightened One's special qualities, <Buddha's virtues> {3 kinds: Vism-a 217}

buddha-ñāṇa—Enlightened One's knowledge {14 kinds: Paṭis I 133; II 31}

buddha-dhamma—Enlightened One's idea, <Buddha's quality> {6 kinds: Vism-a 208}

buddhi—(1) enlightenment, discretion; (2) intelligence: Vism 101

***buddhi**—recognition: Vism-a 134

buddhi-carita—intelligent temperament

***budha**—possessed of wit: Vism 136; Khuddas 20; M-a I 39, 129

bundi—(in *aggijalanasalākābundi*): (goldsmith's) fire-lighting twig-faggot (?) (alternative reading—*panti*): Khp-a 50 (cf. PED *bundika*)

bojjhaṅga—enlightenment factor (7: M II 12, 14; S V 110) [def. Vism-a 128-29; M-a I 82]

bodhi—enlightenment [def. M-a I 54]

bodhipakkhiya-dhamma—idea <state> partaking of enlightenment {5 kinds: S V 227; 14 kinds: Vism 680-1}

bodhisatta—bodhisatta, creature pledged to enlightenment, <being who has vowed to become a Buddha>

by-—*see* also *vy-*

***byañjana**—particle: Vibh-a 387 (= *nipāta*: Vibh-mṭ)

***byañjana-buddhi**—<augmenting of a syllable> {10-fold: M-a II 253}

***byatti**—*see*: *vyatti*

***byabhicarati**—to be an exception, to be irregular: Vism-a (gram.)

***byabhicāra**—exception, irregularity: Vism 441 (gram.)

***byasati**—to ruin: Vibh-a 102

***byāpanicchā**—repetition, reduplication (gram.): Vism-a 229, 407

byāpanna-citta—with mind affected by ill will

byāpāda—*see*: *vyāpāda*

byābajjha—(*a*-) (non-) affliction

byābādha—affliction

byāma—measure of length (head to foot)

byāvaṭa—*see*: *vyāvaṭa*

brahma—divine, perfect, life

brahmacariya—(1) the life divine, <the holy life>, chastity {2 kinds: Vism 214}

***brahmañña**—lover of brahmans: D III 74

brahmabhavana—realm of a (Brahmā) Divinity {10-fold: M-a I}

brahmaloka—world of the (Brahmā) Divinity {9 *brahmaloka-deva*: Vibh 424; 19 *brahmaloka*, 20 *brahmaloka*: M-a II 333}

brahmavihāra—divine abiding (the 4)

brahmā—Divinity, Brahmā Divinity [def. M-a I 34; Vism-a 307]

brāhmaṇa—one belonging to the divine caste, a divine, a brahman {3 kinds: Vism-a 307; 5 b.- *aṅga*: D I 119} [def. M-a I 109; II 418; III 443]

brūhana—intensification

BH

bhaṅga—dissolution

***bhañjati**—to gather (flowers): M-a III 247

***bhaṭṭha**—ground up (*-dhañña*): Khuddas 85

***bhatta**—biscuit (?): Khuddas 87

bhatta—meal {2 kinds: M-a II 208; 14 kinds: Vism 66; Vism A 307}

***bhattar**—(1) employer: Vism 150; (2) employee: M II 123

***bhattavant**—(1) possessed of cultivation (of seclusion, etc.): Vism 212; (2) possessed of devotees: Vism-a 214

bhabba—capable, able

bhaya—(1) fear, terror, cause of fear, fearful {3 kinds: Vibh 367; 5 kinds: S V 387; Vibh 379}; (2) famine (4 *abhayassa bhayanti*: M-a IV 22)

bhayat'upaṭṭhāna—appearance as fearful (stage in insight)

***bhayānaka**—*also* fearing: Vibh 367

bhava—being, becoming, existence {2 kinds: Vibh 137; 3 kinds: M I 50; 6 kinds: Vism 573; 9 kinds: Vibh 137; 24 kinds: Vism 573} [def. M I 50; Vibh 136,145; Vism 528, 571, 576]

bhavaṅga—the "factor of being," life-continuum consciousness (Paṭṭh 159, 160, 169, 322; no Piṭaka ref. in PED)

bhavati—to be, to become, to exist (= *hoti*)

***bhavantara**—the immediately-next existence upon rebirth

bhava-sāta—attraction in being

***bhavyatā (bhabbatā)**—(*sakkhi-*) ability to be a witness: M III 96

***bhavya-rūpatā**—apparent ability: A I 189

***bhāti**—brother (compound stem): Vism 654

bhāra—burden {18 kinds: Vibh-a 388}

bhāva—(1) essence, state, -ness (sometimes used in Commentaries to replace verb hoti); (2) sex; (3) substantive-essence (gram.): Khp-a 106, 224

***bhāva-taddhita**—gerundial derivative (abstr. + suffix *-tā, -tta, (ṇ)ya*) (gram.)

***bhāva-napuṃsaka**—neuter gender abstract noun (gram.)

manāpa—agreeable
manāyatana—mind base [def. Dhs 65; Vibh 71; Vism 481]
mano—loosely—mind; technically—mind (as *manāyatana, manodhātu*, etc.) [def. Dhs 17; Dhs-a 87; M I 295]
manodhātu—mind element [def. Vibh 88; Vism 456, 484]
manopavicāra—mental approach {18 kinds: M III 216}
manoviññāṇa—mind-consciousness
manoviññāṇa-dhātu—mind-consciousness element {68 kinds: Vism 588} [def. Vibh 89-90; Vism 456, 484; Dhs 68]
mantheti—to churn: Vibh-a 141
mamatta—fondness, <possessiveness> {2 kinds: Nidd I 49}
maraṇa—death {2 kinds: Vism 502} [def. D II 305; Vism 229, 502]
mariyāda—barrier, dam, embankment {2 kinds: M-a IV 89}
***marisayati**—to believe (?): M-a III 298
***marisāna**—(*a*-) (dis-) belief (?): M-a III 298
maru—*also* cliff: Vism 531
mala—stain {3 kinds: A I 105; 4 kinds: Vin II 295-96; 8 kinds: A IV 195} [def. Vism 684]
mahagatta—exalted, enlarged (i.e., consciousness exalted from the *kāmāvacara-bhūmi* to the *rūpāvacara-bhūmi* or to the *arūpāvacara-bhūmi* by practice of jhāna and also enlarged in the area of its awareness at that time)
***mahacca**—great pomp: D I 49; M II 65; D-a I 148
mahatta—greatness {2 kinds: Nidd I 49}
***mahamahādivasa**—festival: Vibh-a 474
mahākaruṇā-kāra—act of the great compassion {89: Paṭis-a277}
mahākula—great family, great clan {3 kinds: M-a I 168, i.e., *khattiyamahāsāla, brāhmaṇamahāsāla, gahapatimahāsāla*} [def. Vibh-a 518]
mahādīpa—continent
mahānadī—principal river {the 5: Vism 416}

mahāniraya—principal hell {the 8: Vism 300}

***mahāpadesa**—principal authority {the 4: D II 123} (see PED under *padesa*, though does not the compound resolve into *mahā* + *apadesa*?)

mahāpariccāga—the great relinquishment {the 5: M-a I 45}

mahāpurisa-anubyañjana—details of a Great Man {80: Vism 234; cf. MN Sutta 91}

mahāpurisa-vitakka—thought of a Great Man {the 7 & the 8: A IV 229}

mahābhaya—great fear {16: Vibh 376 and Vibh-a }

mahābhūta—great entity (great primary element of *rūpa*, i.e., *paṭhavī, āpo, tejo, vāyo*) [def. see *bhūta*]

mahāmaṅgala—great blessing {the 5: Vin-a 1008}

mahāvatta—principal duty {80: M-a III 30}

mahāvitakka—principal thought {9 kinds: M-a I 82; see Vibh 355}

mahāvipassanā—principal insight {the 18: Vism 628, 694; see Paṭis I 20}

mahāsandhi—principal joint of the body {14: Vism 185}

mahāsamudde acchariya-abbhuta-dhamma—wonderful and marvellous ideas <qualities> connected with the great ocean {the 8: Ud 53}

mahāsara—great lake {the 7: Vism 416, 650; A IV 101; M-a III 135}

mahāsilā—great rock {the 7: Vism 206}

mahicchatā—greatness of wishes [def. Vibh 351]

***mahī**—*also* greatness (*puñña-*): M I 236

mātikā—(1) schedule; (2) Code (term for *Pātimokkha*. *dve mātikā*—term for *Bhikkhu-* and *Bhikkhunī Pātimokkha*), summary manual (e.g., the *Khuddasikkhā* as a summary of the Vinaya), etc. [def. Vism-a 17]

māna—conceit (pride: connected etymologically with *māneti*—to honour, and semantically with *maññati*—to conceive a conceit) {3 kinds: A III 445; 7 kinds: Vibh 383; 9 kinds: Vibh 389; 18 kinds: Vibh 346} [def. Vibh 355; M-a I 170]

mānasa—notion, mind, thought: M II 262; M-a I 40

māyā—deceit, magic

Māra—Māra {2: Vism 612; 5: Vism 211}

***māḷaka**—(*vitakka-*) debating lodge (*"kattha nu kho ajja bhikkhāya caritabbanti ādinā vitakka-māḷake"*: Vism-a): Vism 342; M-a II 284; III 149

micchatta—wrongness {the 8 and the 10} [def. Vism 683]

micchā—wrong {2 kinds: A I 90}

micchā-diṭṭhi—wrong view {20 kinds: M-a I 73; II 360}

***miḍhi**—shelf, plinth: Khuddas 74; Vin II 113

middha—drowsiness (torpor)

***milāpana**—withering, causing to wither: Vism 461

***missaka-samāsa**—mixed compound (gram.)

mukha—(1) mouth, face; (2) paragraph, heading; (3) way (*mukhena*—by way of: Vism 346); (4) *mukham oloketi*—to pander to: M-a IV 73; (5) *mukha-vaṭṭi*—wall-plate (in architecture): Dhs-a 107

muccitukamyatā—desire for deliverance (stage in insight)

***muṭṭhi**—measure of length (from elbow to knuckles of closed fist)

***muṭṭhi-potthaka**—handbook, pocketbook: M-a II 91

muta—sensed (i.e., smelt, tasted or touched) [def. M-a I 37]

muttā—pearl (see Ud-a 302 and M-ṭ I 73)

muditā—(altruistic) gladness [def. Vibh 274; Vism 318]

mudu—malleable

mudutā—malleability (of *citta* and *kāya*)

***munāti**—to measure (exegesis of *mano*): Vism 481

musā—false

musā-vāda—false speech, lying

***muhuṃ**—(adv.) gradually: S I 110

mūla—(1) root (of plant); (2) root (cause, origin) [def. M-a I 12]

mūla-pada—root-word (18: Nett 2)

***metabba**—must be measured (absol. of *mināti*): Vin I 94

mettā—lovingkindness; *-cetovimutti*—deliverance of mind through *mettā* {3 kinds: Paṭis II 130} [def. Vibh 273; Vism 318]

methuna-saṃyoga—sexual bond {the 7: see A IV 54-56}

***mehana**—Vism 212 (= organ of generation according to Abh)

moha—delusion [def. Dhs 1061; Vibh 362; Vism 468]

Y

***yajrabbeda**—the Yajur Veda: M-a III 362

yañña—sacrifice {5 kinds: A-a }

yaṭṭhi—(1) pole; (2) measure of length (7 *ratana* = 1 y.; 20 y. = 1 *usabha*. Also 4 y. = 1 *abbhantara*; 4 *hattha* = 1 y.)

yathākammūpaga-ñāṇa—knowledge of creatures' <beings'> passing on according to actions

yathānusandhi—*see under*: *anusandhi*

***yathāyogaṃ**—(adv.) following the order stated: Vism 474

***yāna**—*also* footwear, sandals: M-a III 222

***yānar**—one who gains his keep: M II 123

yāmayantanāḷika—stick contrivance for telling the time

***yāva**—*also* measure of length (8 y. = 1 *aṅgula*)

***yuga**—*also* measure of length (1 y. = 9 *vidatthi*)

yuga-naddha—coupling, coupled (of *samatha* and *vipassanā*)

yugala—pair {8: Paṭis-a167}

yugalaka—pair {the 6: i.e., *kāya-* and *citta-passaddhi*, etc.}

yebhuyyena—(adv.) mostly, generally

ye-vā-pana-ka—or whatever state (commentarial term for *saṅkhārā* besides those specified in Dhs § 1 and referred to there by the words *ye vā pana*)

yoga—bond (the 4) [def. Vism 684]

***yogita**—impalement: Vism 611

yojana—measure of lenth, league (between 3 and 7 miles) (4 *gāvuta* = 1 y.; 68,000 y. = Mt. Sineru's height)

yoni—(1) womb; (2) generation, mode of birth (the 4);(3) reason, cause, source (*see*: *ayoni*)

yoniso—with ordered reasoning, <methodical, wise> (*yoniso manasikāra*—reasoned attention)

R

***raṭṭhiya**—governor: Vibh-a 487 (= *raṭṭhika*)

raṇa—conflict (*araṇa*—non-conflict; see M III 235) [def. Dhs-a 50]

ratana—jewel, treasure {2 kinds: A I 94; 3 kinds: = Buddha, Dhamma, Saṅgha; 5 kinds: A III 240: 7 kinds: D II 16; 10 kinds: *see* Ud 56}

ratana—measure of length (2 *vidatthi* = 1 r.; 7 r. = 1 *yaṭṭhi*)

rati—delight

ratha—chariot {2 kinds: M-a II 194}

rathareṇu—measure of length (36 *tajjāri* = 1 r.; 36 r. = 1 *likhā*)

rasa—(1) taste, flavour {6 kinds: Dhs 629}; (2) nature as function (*kicca*) or achievement (*sampatti*); (3) essential juice, filtrate, solution [def. Vism 8, 481]

***rasa**—kind of metal: M-ṭ I 73

***rasaka-dhātu**—*rasa* (metal) ore (?): M-ṭ I 73

***rasati**—to taste: Vism 481

***rasada**—candy: Vibh-a 112

***rasāyana**—elixir, philtre: Vism 568; D-a II 568; Ud-a 399

rāga—lust {3 kinds: M-a II 176}

rājakakudhabhaṇḍa—royal insignia {the 5: M-a IV 185}

***rājī**—*also* a crack: Kkh 74-75

rāmaṇeyyaka—what is delightful {2 kinds: M-a II 250}

ritta—empty, hollow

rukkha—tree {4 kinds: A II 109; 7 kinds: Vism 206}

ruci—preference, opinion

rūpa—form: (1) "material" form (i.e., *rūpakkhandha*); (2) "visible" form (i.e., *rūpāyatana*); (3) *-rūpa* (encl.) <having the quality of> [def. S III 47, 59, 86; Dhs 583f.; Vibh 1, 12, 136; Vism 443f.; D III 217; M III 17]

***rūpa**—stem of verb, etc. (gram.)

rūpa-kalāpa—form-group (i.e., *aṭṭhaka, navaka* and *dasaka; not* object of *kalāpa-sammasana*, q.v.)

rūpa-kāya—the form ("physical") body

rūpa-kkhandha—form aggregate (for def. *see*: *rūpa*)

rūpa-dhātu—form element (as opposed to *kāma-* and *arūpa-*)

rūpa-bhava—being which is accompanied by form (as opposed to *kāma-* and *arūpa-*)

***rūpayati**—is (visibly) formed: Vism 481

***rūpa-rūpa**—concrete form (= *parinipphanna-rūpa* as distinct from *pariccheda-rūpa, ākāra-rūpa* and *vikāra-rūpa*): Vism 590

rūpa-saṅgaha—<classification of form> {3 kinds: D III 217}

rūpāyatana—form base [def. Dhs 617]

rūpāvacara—frequenting form, belonging to the form sphere, the form sphere

rūpin—having form

L

lakkhaṇa—characteristic {2 kinds: Paṭis II 179; 3 kinds: 5, 10 and 50 kinds: Paṭis I 54-57}

***lakkhaṇa-rūpa**—matter as characteristic: Vism 451

***laghimā**—lightness: Vism 211

***lavitta**—(fr. *luṇāti*) reaped harvest: M-ṭ III

lahutā—lightness (of *citta* and *kāya*)
lābha—gain {5 kinds: M-a II 148}
***likhā**—measure of length (36 *rathareṇu* = 1 l.; 7 l. = 1 *ūkā*)
liṅga—(1) mark; (2) sex; (3) gender (gram.)
***liṅgika**—(name) denoting a mark: Vism 210; Khp-a 107
***litta**—(pp. *limpati*) smeared, plastered: Khuddas-a 22
***lega**—string, cord: Dhs-a 90
***lesa**—*also* part, fraction: M-a II 126 (= *apadesa* M-ṭ): Vism-a 828
loka—world {1-18 kinds: Paṭis I 122} [def. S IV 52; Vibh 195, 252; Vism 204; Dhs-a 47]
lokapālaka-dhamma—world-guarding ideas <states> (i.e., the 2, *hiri* and *ottappa*: see A I 51)
lokavāda-paṭisaṃyutta-diṭṭhi—view associated with theories about the world {8 kinds: M-a I 182}
lokiya—mundane, belonging to the world; *lokiya-citta*—mundane consciousness {81 kinds: Vism 588}; *lokiya-pariññā*—mundane full knowledge {3 kinds: Vism 606}; *lokiya-vipassanā*—mundane insight {7 kinds: D-a 531}
lokuttara—supramundane, beyond the world (the meaning given in PED as equivalent of "highest in the world" = *lokagga* seems without any foundation); *lokuttara-citta*—<supramundane consciousness> {8 kinds}; *lokuttarā-dhammā*—<supramundane state> {the 9: Dhs 1094; the 37 = the 37 *bodhipakkhiya-dhamma*}; *lokuttara-vipassanā*—supramundane insight {2 kinds: D-a 331}
***loṇi**—sea: M-a V 73
lobha—greed [def. Dhs 389; Vibh 361; Vism 468]

V

***vaṃsa**—*also* ridge-pole of roof (?): M-a II 50
***vaca**—in compounds *dubbaca* and *suvaca*, q.v.

vacana—designation, word: *taṃ-vacana*—indirect speech (refers to enclitic *iti*): Khp-a 19

***vacanattha**—<word-meaning> (= *saddattha*): Vism 535 (cf. *vacanīyattha*)

***vacanāvayava**—member of syllogism (log.): Vism 532

***vacanīyattha**—meaning or thing verbalized: Vism-a 586 (cf. *saddattha*)

vacī-duccarita—verbal misconduct {the 4 kinds}

***vacī-bheda**—breaking into speech, speech utterance: Vism 448

vacī-saṅkhāra—verbal determination, <verbal formation> (i.e., *vitakka-vicāra*)

vacī-sucarita—verbal good conduct

vajja—censurable {2 kinds: A I 47}

vaṭṭa—round (e.g., *kamma-*, *vipāka-*, *kilesa-*, as aspects of the wheel of being [*bhavacakka*]); term for dependent origination as arising (opp. of *vivaṭṭa*)

vaḍḍhana—extension, increase {2 *vaḍḍhana-bhūmi*: Vism 152}

vaṇijjā—trade {5 kinds: A III 208}

***vaṇita**—inflated: Vism 183

vaṇṇa—(1) colour {5 kinds: Vin III 112}; (2) appearance; (3) caste

***vaṇṇa**—*also* syllable: Vism 211; Khp-a 107

vata—duty, vow (see also: *sīlabbata*)

vatta—duty (see also: *mahā-*) (i.e., to preceptor, etc.)

***vattana**—performance of duties (to preceptor, etc.): Vism 100; Vin I 61

***vattana**—act of saying: M-a to M II 228

***vattamāna-kāla**—present tense (gram.)

vattuṃ—inf. of *vatti* (= *vadati*): M-a III 222

***vattha**—corn: Vibh-a 445; Vism 216

***vatthika**—clothable: Vism 216

vatthu—(1) land, ground; (2) basis, physical basis, organ; (3) (heart-) basis (= *hadaya-vatthu*); (4) object; (5) instance, example; (6) story

***vatthuṃ**—inf. of *vasati*

***vatthu-dasaka**—physical-basis decad (serving for *mano-viññāṇa* as *cakkhu-dasaka* serves for *cakkhu-viññāṇa*): Vism 128

***vatthu-rūpa**—*rūpa* belonging to the heart-basis: Vism-a 367

vana—grove {2 kinds: M-a I 11}

vappa—sowing (of crops) {2 kinds: S-a I 242}

vaya—fall (see also: *udaya*), disappearance

vaya (vayo)—stage of life {the 3: Vism 619; 3 *-kkhandha*: Nd.2}

***varanaka**—a plait (? of straw): A-a

***varāhadāṭha**—kind of pearl: M-ṭ I 73

***varitatta**—(abstract) fr. *varāti* (*vuṇāti*) restrainedness: M-a I 140

valāhaka—(1) thundercloud {4 kinds: A II 102}; (2) the name of "Horse Treasure" (*assa-ratana*: M III 174)

***valāhakajā**—kind of pearl: M-ṭ I 73

vavaṭṭhāna—defining

vasa—mastery; *vasena* (either encl. or with gen. in commentarial usage = instrumental case) (1) through, by means of; (2) as

vasa-vattana—(susceptible to) exercise of mastery (in definition of *anattā*)

vasi—mastery {5 kinds: Paṭis I 99}

vācā—speech {4 kinds: see M I 345} [def. Vibh 105; Vism 509; Dhs-a 86]

vāta—wind, air

vāditā—telling: M III 29

***vāna**—fastening: Vism 293

vāyāma—effort [def. D II 312; Dhs 12; Vibh 105, 107; Vism 510]

vāyo—air [def. M I 422; Vibh 84; Vism 350-52, 363, 365; Vism-a 359]

vāra—(1) turn; (2) instance, case; (3) section, sub-section

***vāvaṭa (vyāvaṭa, byāvaṭa)**—turned towards, involved: M-a IV 178; Vibh-a 313, 475

***vāhanika**—float, catamaran: Vism 561; Vibh-a 171

***vikappa**—alternative: Vism 365; M-a I 67; ambiguity: M-a II 126

***vikappana**—(1) suggestion: M-a I 94; (2) transference (of one of the 4 requisites to someone else): Vin IV 122

vikampati—to shake, to waver

vikampana—shaking, wavering

vikāra—alteration, alterability

***vikāra-rūpa**—*rūpa* as alteration (term for certain kinds of *rūpa*, e.g., *aniccatā*): Vism 451

***vikuppati**—to be damaged: Vism 706

vikubbana—(1) versatility (in development of *brahma-vihāra*); (2) transformation (by *iddhi-vidha*)

vikkhambhana—suppression (of *nīvaraṇa* by *samatha*)

vikkhepa—distraction (*a-* used in def. of *samādhi*)

***vigaccha**—hideous (= *virūpa*: Vism-a): Vism 652 (is this a reading for *bībaccha*?)

vighāta—annoyance

vicāra—(1) exploring; (2) (mentally) exploring, pondering (1 of the 5 *jhānaṅga*) {6 kinds: Paṭis I 6} [def. Dhs 8; Vism 142]

***vicāraka**—helper: Vism 65

vicikicchā—uncertainty {5-fold: Vism 599; 6-fold: Vism 599; 8 kinds: Vibh 364; M-a I 73} [def. M I 275; Dhs 425; Vibh 364; Vism 471]

***vicchikālika—out of season**—M-a IV

***vijambhati**—to stretch, to yawn: Vism 311

vijānana—act of cognizing

vijānāti—to cognize

vijjati—to exist, to be found, to be possible (lit. is known)

vijjatisāri—*read*: *vippaṭisāri*: M-a V 9

vijjamāna—factual, existent, possible

vijjā—(1) true knowledge {the 3 and the 8}; (2) science

viññatti—intimation, communication [def. Dhs 636-37; Vism 447-48]

viññāṇa—consciousness {6 kinds: M I 53; 81 kinds: Vism 588; 89 kinds: Vism 457; 121 kinds: Abhidh-s Pt 1} [def. M I 53; II 17; III 17, 242; S III 47, 61, 87; M I 111; Dhs 63; Vibh 9, 53; Vism 452f., 528]

viññāṇa-kāya—body of consciousness {the 6}

viññāṇa-ṭṭhiti—foundation for consciousness {the 4: D III 228; the 7: D III 253}

viññāṇa-dvāra—door of consciousness {the 5: Dhs-a 95}

viññāṇa-dhātu—consciousness element

viññāṇa-ppavatti-ākāra—mode of occurrence of consciousness {the 14: Vism 457}

viññāta—cognized (i.e., by the *mano*: in expression *diṭṭha-suta-muta-viññāta*)

***viṭabhi**—canopy: M I 306 (*not* as in PED)

vitakka—thought {3 kinds: A I 275; 6 kinds: Vibh 346; Paṭis I 6} [def. Dhs 7; Vism 142; Vism-a 138] *see also: mahā-* and *mahā-purisa-*

vitakkana—thinking, act of thinking

vitakka-māḷaka—*see māḷaka*

***vitiṇṇa**—*also* wide: Khuddas-a 74

***vitthambhana**—distension (in definition of *vāyo-dhātu*): Vism 352 (cf. *rūpassa thambhitatta* in description of *vāyo* at Vibh 84, also *samudīraṇa* as other def. of *vāyo*)

vitthāra—detail

vidatthi—span (measure of length: 12 *aṅgula* = 1 v.; 2 v. = 1 *ratana*; 1 *sugatavidatthi* = 3 v.)

***vidhi**—*also* invitation: Vism 216

***vidheyya**—to be arranged: Vism 252

***vinana**—joining together: Vism 293

vinaya—(1) removal, discipline, leading away (discipline by leading away faults); (2) the Vinaya, 1st book of the Tipiṭaka {2 kinds: M-a I 22; II 208; 10 kinds: M-a I 22} [def. M-a I 22]

***vinicchaya**—definition, exposition {4 kinds: Vibh-a 512}

***viniddhuta**—shaken off: Vibh-a

***viniddhunaka**—which shakes off: Vibh-a 121

***viniddhunaṇa**—shaking off: Vism 510

***viniddhunāti**—to shake off: Vism 510 (= *viddhaṃsati*: Vism-a)

vinipāta—perdition

***vinibbedha**—diameter: M-a IV 220

vinibbhoga—resolution (of compact into elements): M-a I 242

***vinivāraṇa**—holding back: Khp-a 185

***vipakkamati**—to go away: M III 148

***vipacita**—spelling of *vipañcita*: Vism-a 224

vipañcita—expanded (meaning)

***vipañceti**—to expand (meanings): Vism-a 225

vipatti—unsuccess, failure {2 kinds: D III 21; 3 kinds: A I 268, 270}

viparāmosa—brigandage {2 kinds: M-a II 211}

vipariṇāma—change

vipariṇāma-dukkha—suffering (pain) due to change

***vipariyāsa**—*cetaso-* out of one's mind, <mental derangement>: M II 248

vipariyesa—perverseness

vipallāsa—perversion {3 kinds: A II 52} [def. Vism 683]

vipassati—to see with insight, to have insight into

vipassanā—insight (primarily into the 3 *lakkhaṇa* of *anicca, dukkha* and *anattā*) {3 kinds: Vism 705; 4 kinds: Paṭis I 58} [def. Dhs 55]

vipassanā-yānika—one whose vehicle is insight
vipassanūpakkilesa—imperfection of insight {the 10: Paṭis II 100; Vism 633}
vipāka—ripening, result (of action)
vipāka-vaṭṭa—the round of ripening of action {5-fold: Vism 579, 600; M-a IV 65}
vipāka-viññāṇa—consciousness as ripening of action, kamma-resultant consciousness
***vipekkhati**—to look to one side: M II 137
vippayutta—dissociated
***vipphandana**—*also* excitement: Vism 278
vipphandita—vacillation (of views)
***vipphāra**—*also* intervention: Paṭis II 211; Vism 142, 378, 462 (= *vega*: Paṭis-a36; = *vyāpāra*: Vism-a 484)
***vipphāravant**—possessing intervention: Vism 142
***vibuddha**—awakened: Khp-a 15
***vibhagga**—coming unstuck: M-a IV 183
vibhaṅga—(1) analytical exposition; (2) 2nd book of the Abhidhamma-piṭaka in 18 parts
***vibhatta**—built, constructed (?): M-a I 15
***vibhatti**—inflexion, declension, personal suffix of verb and case-ending of noun (gram.)
vibhava—(1) non-being, non-becoming, <destruction>; (2) success
***vibhāvita**—explained: M-a III 350; Dhs-a 55
***vimaṭṭa**—smooth (= *vimaṭṭha*)
***vimaddha**—smooth (= *vimaṭṭha*): M II 13
vimuttāyatana—base for deliverance {5 kinds: A III 21}
vimutti—deliverance {2 kinds: Paṭis II 143; 5 kinds: M-a IV 168}
vimutti-paripācana-saññā—perception ripening in deliverance {5 kinds: D III 243}

vimokkha—liberation {3 kinds: Vism 658; 8 kinds: M II 12; 68 kinds: Paṭis II 168; 75 kinds: Paṭis-a385}
vimokkha-mukha—gateway to liberation {the 3: Paṭis II 48}
***vimhaya**—*also* hypothetical: M-a II 284
***vimhāpana**—*also* hypocrisy
***viyoga**—disjunction (i.e., the word *vā*) (gram.)
***viyojeti**—to separate: Vism 252
virajjati—to fade away, to cause fading of lust (*rāga*)
virati—abstinence: M III 74; Sn 264 {2 kinds: Vism-a 21; 3 kinds: M-a I 203; Khp-a 142}
viramaṇa—abstaining
***viraha**—(subst.) absence: Vism 158
virahita—devoid of, destitute of
virāga—fading, fading away of lust {2 kinds: Vism 290}
viriya—energy (*caturaṅga*-v.: M-a I 124; II 257: refers to phrase *kāmaṃ taco ca nahārū ca aṭṭhi ca avasissatu sarīre upasussatu maṃsalohitaṃ* (S II 28) according to M-ṭ) [def. S V 197; Dhs 13; Vism 464]
viriyārambha-vatthu—basis for arousing energy (the 7)
***virodha**—*also* conflict, contradiction (log.) {6 *virodha-vatthu*: Vibh 380}
***vilīmaṃsa**—(*so read for*: *cilīma* at M III 274) flesh just under the skin (*vilīmaṃsan ti cammanissitamaṃsaṃ*: M-ṭ III): M III 274
***vilopeti**—to haul (*maccha*): A III 31
vivaṭṭa—(1) cessation of the round (*see*: *vaṭṭa*); (2) turning away (stage in insight); (3) expansion of *loka* after *saṃvaṭṭa*, q.v.
vivitta—secluded
viveka—seclusion {4 kinds: Vism-a 114; 5 kinds: M-a I 85}
***visaṅketa**—failure of rendezvous: Khuddas-a 122
visaṅkharoti—to analyse (= *vibhajati*: Vism-a): Vism 623
visada—(1) clean; (2) clear-cut, definite

visaya—(1) abode, habitat; (2) objective field (term for 6 *bāhirāyatana*); (3) subject-matter discussed

***visayin**—possessor of objective field (term for 6 *ajjhattikāyatana*): Vism-a

***visavana**—displaying, production: Khp-a 15

***visavitā**—burgeoning (alternative readings: *vikasitā, visatitā*): Paṭis I 174; II 206; Vism 384; Dhs-a 109 (= *arahatā*: As-mṭ 84; Khp-a 14-15)

***visahati**—to suffer, to bear: Vism 69

***visādana**—dejection: Vism 504

***visārin**—rambling (*a*-): M II 140

***visikhā-kathā**—talk about streets (not as in PED; see M-a III 223)

visuddhi—purification {7 kinds: MN Sutta 24; 9 kinds: D III 288}

visūka—distortion

***vissaṭṭhi**—indolence (?): A IV 52 (see PED *visaṭṭhi*)

***vihaṭamāna**—being carded: Vism 657 (= *vihaññamāna*: Vism-a)

***vihata**—beaten: D II 141

***vihata**—spread out, stretched out (*su*-): M III 105

viharati—to abide, to dwell [def. M-a I 10]

vihāra—(1) dwelling place, abode; (2) monastery (18 *vihāra-dosa*: Vism 118); (3) (mode of) abiding {3 kinds: D III 220; Vism-a 211}

vihiṃsā—cruelty

***vītaccika**—without flame (*vi* + *ita* + *acci* + *ka*): D II 133

***vītiharaṇa**—*also* shifting sideways: Vism 621; M-a I 260

vīthi—(1) street; (2) (*citta*-) cognitive series (in the occurrence of consciousness): Vism 22

vīthi-citta—consciousness belonging to the cognitive series

***vīna**—weaving (= *vāyana*): M-ṭ III 410

***vībaccha**—*reading for*: *bībaccha*

vīmaṃsaka—inquirer {2 kinds: M-a II 387; 3 kinds: M-a II 378}

vīmaṃsā—inquiry

vuṭṭhāti—to emerge, <to be rehabilitated>

vuṭṭhāna—(1) emergence (from a meditative attainment); (2) <rehabilitation (from an *āpatti*)>

vuṭṭhānagāminī-vipassanā—insight leading to emergence (of the path)

***vuḍḍha**—half (= *aḍḍha*): Vism 622

vutta—said (*idaṃ vuttaṃ hoti*—"this is what is meant": common commentarial idiom introducing paraphrases; *vuttaṃ h'etaṃ*—"for this is said": *as above* introducing a quotation)

***vuddha**—increased (= *vaḍḍhita*): M II 165

vuddhi—increase {2 kinds: A I 94}

***vuyhati**—*see*: *uyhati*

***vekurañjāya—(?): M II 153 (Be suggests *vekulaso* (adv.)—** belonging to no clan)

vega—urgency, need

veda—(1) inspiration, joy; (2) wisdom; (3) the Vedas

vedaka—one who feels

vedanā—feeling (only in the narrow sense of pleasure, pain, and neither) {2 kinds: M I 397; 3 kinds: D III 216; Vism 460; 4 kinds: Vibh 405; 5 kinds: Vism 461; 6 kinds: see M I 302-3; 6 kinds: Paṭis I 6; 7 kinds: Vibh 401; 8 kinds: S IV 230; see also MN Sutta 59 [def. M I 51, 89, 293, 302, 397; S III 47, 59, 86; IV 204f.; Dhs 3, 60, 415, 433; Vibh 3, 15, 130; Vism 460, 528; Dhs-a 41, 109]

vedanā-kāya—feeling body {the 6: M I 51}

vedanānupassanā—contemplation of feeling {9 kinds: D II 298; M I 59}

vedayita—what is felt, feeling

vedīyati—to feel, to be felt

vedeti—to feel

***vedeyya**—what experiences: M I 8, 258

venayika—one who leads away, who disciplines (*see*: *vinaya*: there is a pun here made at Vin III 3; cf. M I 140), nihilist, discipliner; also one who has to be led away, got rid of (A-a to A V 190)

***veyyābādhika**—*also* causing affliction: M I 10 (see M-a)

veramaṇī—abstention {5 kinds: see A IV 220} [def. M-a I 203]

velā—time, season [def. M-a II 95]

***veḷuja**—kind of pearl: M-ṭ I 73

vesārajja—intrepidity {4 kinds: M I 71-72}

***vessantara**—beyond temptation, <crossed over entirely (?)> M I 386 (M-a: *rāgādivisamaṃ* [M-ṭ *rāgādivisaṃ*] *taritvā vitaritvā ṭhito*)

vokāra—constituent (*eka-vokāra-bhava*: one-constituent being, i.e., *rūpa*, only as *asaññi*; *catu-*: four-c.-b., i.e., the *arūpa-bhava* with the 4 *nāma-kkhandha; pañca-*: five-c.-b., i.e., rest of *rūpa-bhava* and *kāma-bhava* with all 5 *khandha*)

voṭṭhapana—determining (consciousness: one of the members of the *citta-vīthi*)

vodāna—cleansing (technically the consciousness that precedes *appanā* or *magga*)

vosāna—stopping halfway

***vosāsana**—instruction, education: Khp-a 241

vossagga—relinquishment {2 kinds: M-a I 85; II 299}

vohāra—(1) commerce, trade; (2) communication, term, way of speech; (3) common usage

vy—*see also*: *by-*

vyañjana—(1) sauce; (2) consonant (gram.), syllable; (3) detail

***vyatireka**—negative, negation (log., gram.)

***vyatti**—particular distinction: Vism 214; (= *viyatti* and *veyyatti*): M-a I 6; Paṭis-a430

***vyatti**—extension, pervasion (synonym for *pharati* in logical sense), concomitance (of *sādhya* & *hetu* in syllogism) (log.)

vyappanā—fixity: M III 73 (no sutta ref. in PED)
***vyappita**—gone away (*vi* + *apa* + *ita*): Vibh 258; Vism 157
vyasana—ruin {10 kinds: A V 169}
***vyasanīyatā**—malpractice (*a*-): Khp-a 139
***vyākaraṇa**—*also* prose (gram.)
***vyādāna**—averting, turning away (*mukhaṃ vyādāya sayati*: Vism-a)
vyāpaka—*also* (1) coextensive, spreading throughout (Vism 211, 447); (2) concomitant (log.)
***vyāpajjitar**—one who undertakes: M III 127
***vyāpanna**—*also* (adj. fr. *vyāpāda*) with mind of ill will (*-citta*)
vyāpāda—ill will [def. M I 275-76; Dhs 419]
***vyāpāra**—*also* interest, interestedness: Vism 585, 595

S

sa-—(prefix) (1) with, affected by (= *saha*, e.g., *sāsava*); (2) true (= *sat*, e.g., *sappurisa*); (3) own (= *saka*, e.g., *sabhāva*)
sa-uttara—surpassed (by something else)
saṃ—(1) own (= *sayaṃ*); (2) (= *siyaṃ*: A II 212); Vism-a
saṃyoga—bondage
***saṃyoga**—conjunction (= *sampiṇḍana*, i.e., the words *ca* and *pi* meaning "and") (gram.); *see also*: *accanta-*
saṃyojana—fetter {7 kinds: A IV 7, 8; Vibh 383; 11 kinds: Paṭis I 143} [def. D III 234; Vibh 361; Vism 682]
saṃyojaniya—provocative of fetters
saṃvaṭṭa—contraction (of *loka*: opp. of *vivaṭṭa*) {3 *saṃvaṭṭa-sīmā*: Vism 414}
***saṃvaṇṇa**—detailing: Khp-a 224
saṃvaṇṇita—*also* in detail: Vism 411 (= *vitthārita*: Vism-a 407); Khp-a 135
***saṃvaṇṇeti**—to detail: Khp-a 224

saṃvara—restraint {5 kinds: M-a I 62; Vism 7; 8 *saṃvara-dvāra*: Dhs-a 95} [def. M-a I 62]
saṃvega—sense of urgency {8 *saṃvega-vatthu*: M-a I 298; Khp-a 235 (PED omits the 8th)}
*__saṃvedanika__—which feels, experiences: Vism 477
saṃsagga—conjoinedness, association {5 kinds: M-a II 143}
saṃsaṭṭha—conjoined, associated
saṃsāra—round of rebirths, roundabout
*__saṃsilesa__—joining, junction, cohesion: M-a I 37
saṃsīdati—to founder
*__saṃhanana__—*also* paralysis: Vism 469 Vism-a 493
saka—own
sakadāgāmin—once-returner (2nd stage of realization)
*__sakalika__—*also* scale (of fish): Vism 250
*__sakkarā__—sugar (= *sakkharā*)
sakkāya—embodiment, <personality> [def. M I 299; II 265]
sakkāya-diṭṭhi—embodiment view, <personality view>
sakkhin—witness, example
sagga—heaven, paradise
*__sagga__—relinquishment: M-a I 190
saṅkanti—transmigration
saṅkappa—intention
saṅkamana—transmigrating
*__saṅkara__—confounding, confusing: Vism 447, 711
*__saṅkalana__—definition: M-a I 2
*__saṅkāmana__—casting (*kusa* grass): Khuddas 95
*__saṅkāmeti__—to cast (*kusa* grass): Khuddas 95
*__saṅkitteti__—to announce, to publish (? in exegesis of *saṅkitti*): M-a II 44
saṅkiliṭṭha—defiled
saṅkilesa—defilement {3 kinds: Vism 4, 5}
saṅkilesika—defiling

***saṅkileseti**—to defile: Dhs-a 42

***saṅkupatha**—*also* a path on piles: Vism 305

saṅkhata—determined, <conditioned, formed> (i.e., not *nibbāna*; 3 *saṅkhata-lakkhaṇa*: A I 152)

saṅkhā—calculation, reckoning [def. M-a I 75]

saṅkhāra—determination, <formation> {3 kinds: M I 301; 6 kinds: Vism 526; 50 kinds: Vism 462f.} [def. D III 217; M I 54, 301; III 17; S III 47, 60, 86; Vism 462f., 528, 530; Vism-a 386; Dhs 62, 398; Vibh 7, 41, 135, 144]

saṅkhāra-kkhandha—determinations <formations> aggregate

saṅkhāra-dukkha—suffering (pain) inseparable from determinations <formations>

saṅkhāra-pariccheda—delimiting of determinations <formations> (preparation for insight)

saṅkhārupekkhā—equanimity about determinations <formations> (last stage of insight before *anuloma*)

***saṅkhya-taddhita**—numerical derivative (gram.)

saṅgati—(1) chance, coincidence; (2) coincidence, coming together

saṅgaha—help {2 kinds: A I 92; 4 kinds: M-a II 218} (4 -*vatthu*: M-a III 165)

***saṅgaha**—*also* (1) postponement (of *pavāraṇā*): M-a II 150; IV 138; (2) holding together (a function of *āpo*): Vism 365; (3) group, collection

***saṅgahita**—held together: Vism 365

saṅgha—community, the Community (of Bhikkhus) (7 *saṅghagata-dakkhiṇa*: see MN 142)

saṅghaṭṭana—impingement, knocking together

sacca—truth, fact {2 kinds: M-a I 138; 3 kinds: Vibh 405; the 4: MN Sutta 141} [def. Vism 494f]

sacca-ñāṇa—knowledge of truth {2 kinds: Vism 510}

saccānulomika-ñāṇa—knowledge in conformity with truth

***saccālika**—distortion of truth: S IV 306; Vibh-a 338

***sacchika**—based on realization: Paṭis I 174

sacchikaraṇīya-dhamma—idea <state> to be realized {4: D III 230}

sacchikaroti—to realize (especially of the 3rd *sacca*)

sacchikiriyā—realization {2 kinds: M-a III 275; 3 kinds: Vism 696}

sañcetanā—choice, <volition>: S II 39-40 {3 kinds: Vism 530}

sañcetanā-kāya—body of choice, <class of volition> {6: D III 244}

sañjānana—act of perceiving

sañjānāti—to perceive

saññā—(1) perception (both as perceiving and percept); (2) label, indicating sign {4 kinds: A V 63; Vibh 405; 5 kinds: A III 79, 85; 7 kinds: Vibh 401; Vism 607; A IV 46; 9 kinds: D III 289; 10 kinds: D III 291; A V 109} [def. M III 17; S III 47, 60, 87; Dhs 4, 61; Vibh 5, 28; Vism 461; Dhs-a 110]

saññā-kāya—body of perception {6: D III 244}

saññā-vimokkha—(1) liberation through perception, <liberation accompanied by perception>: Sn 206 <= 4 jhānas and 3 lower *āruppa*s: Sn-a to Sn v.1072>; <(2) release from a disciplinary offense by not perceiving an action as an offense (Kkh 24)>

saññāvedayitanirodha—cessation of perception and feeling

saññin—percipient

saññivāda—theory of percipience (of self after death)

***saññūḷha**—composed, made up, concocted: M I 386

***saṭhayati**—to defraud: M-a I 189

saṇṭhāna—shape

***saṇṭhāna**—*also* (1) steadying, settling down, stationariness: Vism 88, 245; Vism-a 40; (2) co-presence: Vism 535

sata—mindful

***sata**—*also* remembered (*dussata*: ill-remembered; *sussata*: well-remembered): M I 520

satata-vihārin—one who abides in constant mindfulness and full awareness: M-a IV 70

***sat'asmi**—I am temporary (*sīdatī ti sataṃ, aniccass' etaṃ adhivacanaṃ*: Vibh-a 514): Vibh 392

sati—mindfulness [def. D II 313; S V 197; Dhs 14; Vibh 102; Vism 162, 464, 510]

satipaṭṭhāna—(*sati* + *paṭṭhāna*: M-a I 238; *sati* + *upaṭṭhāna*: Paṭis I 177) foundation of mindfulness, establishment of mindfulness {3 kinds: M III 221; 4 kinds: MN 10} [def. DN 22; Vism 678]

satta—creature, <being> (at S III 190, derived from *sajjati*: to clutch, <but properly derived from *sat*, to exist>)

***satta**—bright principal, *sattva* (of the Sāṃkhya): Vism 310; Vism-a

sattapada—position for beings {the 36: M III 217}

***sattamī**—(1) optative tense; (2) locative case (gram.)

satta-saññā—the seven perceptions (= 1st seven of 18 *mahā-vipassanā*)

satta-saññā—perception of a being

sattāvāsa—abode of beings {the 9: D III 263}

***satthahāraka**—*also* lethal weapon (see M III 266: *satthaṃ āharesi*)

***satthācariya**—arms instructor: M-a II 94

sadda—(1) sound; (2) word, grammar (gram.) {10 kinds: D II 147}

saddattha—word-meaning, dictionary meaning (opp. of *vacanīyattha*, q.v.): Vism-a 586

sadda-navaka—sound ennead (i.e., *aṭṭhaka* + sound)

sadda-lakkhaṇa—grammar (gram.)

sadda-sattha—grammatical science (gram.)

sadda-siddhi—establishment of a word (*see*: *sādhana*)

saddahati—to have faith, to place faith in

saddāyatana—sound base (what is heard)

saddhamma—the true idea, <i.e., (1) the true teaching: M I 404; S II 224; (2) true idea, good quality> {the 4 kinds: A II 47; the 7: D III 252}

saddhā—faith {4 kinds: M-a III 326} [def. S V 197; Dhs 12; Vism 464]

saddhānusārin—mature in faith {6 kinds: M-a III 189; D-a 529}

saddhā-vimutta—liberated by faith {6 kinds: M-a III 189}

***saddheyya**—faith-inspiring: Vism 214

sanidassana—with visibility, visible

***sanidāna**—with sources: M II 9

santati—continuity {2 kinds: Vism 431; 3 kinds: *see*: *ti-santati*; 4 kinds: (*catusantati-rūpa*): Vism-a ; 7 kinds: (*satta-santati-rūpa*): Vism 614}

santati-paññatti—description (concept) of continuity: Pp-a 174

***santati-sīsa**—continuity-heading (term for *dasaka*): Vism 559

santāna—continuity

santi—peacefulness {3 kinds: Nidd I 74}

***san ti**—(= *siyan ti*: see A-a): A II 212

santiṭṭhati—to settle down

santi-pada—state of peacefulness (term for *nibbāna*)

santīraṇa—investigation (consciousness: member of *citta-vīthi*)

santosa—contentment {3 kinds: M-a II 141; 12 kinds: M-a II 211}

***santha**—(in exegesis of *santhāgāra*): M-a III 16

***santhambhati**—to stiffen: Khuddas-a 84

santhambhana—stiffening

***sandana**—flowing: M-a I 80

***sandahana**—*also* connecting, putting together: Dhs-a 112

***sandhāraṇa**—upholding, holding together: Vism 445

sandhi—(1) joint, hinge; (2) liaison (gram.)
*__sannikkhepana__—*also* putting down: Vism 622; M-a I 260
*__sannicchaya__—definition, exposition: Vism 711 (= *vinicchaya*)
sanniṭṭhāna—(1) deciding, conviction (in explanation of *adhimokkha*): Vism 466; (2) decision, decisive pronouncement, deciding action: Dhs-a 88; As-mṭ 75
*__sanniṭṭheyya__—fit to be convinced about: Vism 466
sannipāta—concurrence
*__sannirujjhana__—*also* fixing down: Vism 143, 622
*__sannirumbhana__— = *sannirujjhana*: M-a I 260
*__sanniviṭṭha__—constructed, interpretively constructed: Vism-a 41; Khp-a 232
*__sannivesa__—*also* construction, interpretive construction: Vism-a 41; Khp-a 226
*__sannissaya__—waiting on, dependence: Vism 442
sappa—serpent {3 kinds: Vism-a 48-49}
sappaṭigha—with resistance, <with sensory impingement, said of 5 *indriyas* and their *ārammaṇas*>
*__sappati__—(passive of *sapati*: to swear); to be emitted, spoken; (in exegesis of *sadda*): Vism 481
*__sappadesa__—selective, not inclusive (cf. *nippadesa*): Vism 514; Dhs-a
sappāya—suitable {7 kinds: Vism 127}
sappurisa—true man (7 *sappurisa-dhamma*: D III 252; 8 *sappurisa-dāna*: A IV 243)
sappurisa-paññatti—description of a true man {the 3: A I 151}
sabba—all {2 kinds: It-a I 52; 4 kinds: It-a I 52; S-a II 3} [def. M-a I 17; S IV 15]
*__sabbanāma__—pronoun (gram.)
*__sabbohārika__—normally accepted, ordinary, normal: A-a to A V 196
*__sabbhāva__—(*sat* + *bhāva*) presence: Vism 51; Vibh-a 32

*__sa-bhāva__—with sex: Vism 552

sabhāva—individual essence (Paṭis II 178; see Paṭis-a= *saha-bhāva*: Vism-a 282; or *saka bhāva* or *samāna bhāva*: Vism-a 432)

sabhāva-dhamma—idea <or state> with individual essence (opp. of *asabhāva-dhamma*: an idea <or state> with no individual essence, e.g., *ākāsa, paññatti, saññāvedayitanirodha, rūpassa aniccatā*, etc.)

*__sama__—(1) even, level; (2) righteous: M I 285

*__samacintesuṃ__—aor. 3rd pers. pl. of *sañcinteti*: M I 151

samaṇa—monk {12 kinds: D-a 588} [def. M-a II 4]

samatikkama—surmounting {2 kinds: Vism 111}

samatha—peace (term for *jhāna* and synonym for *samādhi*) {3 kinds: Paṭis-a} [def. Dhs 54]

samatha-vipassanā—peace and insight (the 2 forms of *bhāvanā* which coupled (*yuganaddha*) lead to the path)

samanantara—contiguity, immediate proximity {2 kinds: D-594}

samanupassanā—way of seeing {4 kinds: M-a II 111}

*__samanumajjati__—to work out: M II 247

samanta—(adj.) surrounding: Vism 181

*__samantato__—(adv.) all round: Vism 181

*__samanniṭṭha__—(*su-*) (well) sought: M I 320

*__samanvāneti__—to send after: M III 188

*__samabbhāhata__—*also* (1) stretched out (= *suvihata*): Vism 153; (2) propelled (= *pellana*): Vism 365 Cf. *abbhāhata*

samaya—occasion [def. Dhs-a 57-58; M-a I 7]

*__samavāya__—*also* (1) event: Dhs-a 57; (2) inherence (of cause in effect, according to brahmanical philosophy): Vism 513; Vism-a 753

*__samaveta__—inherent: Vism 513

samasīsin—<one who reaches arahatship simultaneously with the ending of life: Pp 13; Pp-a 186> [3 kinds: S-a I 183; see Paṭis I 101]

samādāna—giving effect to, <undertaking>
samādhāna—coordinating
***samādhāneti**—to cause to put together (?): Khuddas 86
samādhi—concentration {2 kinds: A I 219-20; Vism 85; 3 kinds: D III 219 (twice); Vism 85; Vism 144; 4 kinds: D III 223, 277; Vism 85; 5 kinds: D III 277, 278; Vism 85} [def. D II 313; M I 301; S V 197; Dhs 15; Vibh 105; Vism 84f., 464, 510]
samādhi-cariya—behaviour of concentration {the 9: Paṭis I 99}
samāpatti—attainment {the 9: M I 159-60}
***samāpana**—conclusion (gram.): Vism-a 99
***samāpanna**—one who has attained (e.g., the *āruppāni* by means of *bhāvanā* as opposed to one who has been reborn (*nibbatta*) there): Dhs 1282
samāropana—attribution
***samāropeti**—to attribute: Vism 652
samāsa—compound (gram.)
***samāhata**—brought in, adduced: Vism 166
***samāhāra**—copulative compound with singular termination (gram.)
***samugghāteti**—to abolish: M-a II 368; Vism 370
samuccaya—conjunction (= *sampiṇḍana* and *saṃyoga*) (gram.)
samuṭṭhāna—origination (of *rūpa*) {4 kinds: Vism 614}; (of a Vinaya offence) {6 kinds: Kkh 22-23}
***samuṭṭhāpaya**—rousable: S V 112; Vism 31
samudaya—origin (either as arising or as cause) [def. Vibh 101, 106, 109; Vism 506]
samudācarati—to exercise
samudācaritatta—exercisedness
samudācāra—exercise
samudāciṇṇa—exercised
samudīraṇa—moving (function of *vāyo*)

***samunnāhana**—pressing talk: Vibh 352

***samuppātana**—dissecting away: Khp-a 21

***samullapanā**—*also* flattering talk: Vibh 352

samūha—mass [def. Dhs-a 38]

samūhatā—massiveness

samodahati—to combine

samodhāna—combining

samodhāna-paññatti—collective description (concept): Pp-a 174

sampajañña—full-awareness, full understanding [def. Vism 162; M-a I 253]

sampaṭicchana—receiving (consciousness: member of the *citta-vīthi*)

***sampaṭipādaka**—application (of simile): M-a II 70

***sampaṭipādana**—keeping to the track: Vism 187

***sampatta**—*also* customary: Khp-a 25, 142

***sampatta-virati**—abstinence (by family custom, etc.) from a (temptation) encountered: M-a I 203; Khp-a 25, 32, 142

***sampatta-visaya**—having a contiguous objective field (of *pasāda* other than *cakkhu* and *sota*): Vism 445

sampatti—(1) success; (2) achievement (one of the 2 kinds of *rasa*)

sampadāna—dative case (gram.)

***sampadāna**—(i) making of: Vism 417; (ii) (*piṭaka-*) *also* what is handed down (in the texts): A I 189; M I 520 (reading *sampadāya*):

sampanna—perfected in, <possessed of> {3 kinds: M-a I 153}; *sampann'ajjhāsaya* {2 kinds: Vism-a 112}

sampayutta—associated with

***sampavattati**—to occur: Vism 135

sampasāda—confidence {2 kinds: M-a IV 59}

***sampasādayati**—to make confident: Vism 156

***sampāpanā**—denigrating: Vibh 353

***sampiṇḍana**—*also* conjunction (the words *ca* and *pi*) (gram.) (= *saṃyoga* and *samuccaya*): Khp-a 228

***sampiṇḍeti**—to conjoin (i.e., to perform the function of a conjunction): M-a I 40 (gram.)

***sampekkhāyana**—observation: Paṭis II 197

samphappalāpa—gossip

samphassa—contact

sambuddha—Fully Enlightened One

sambojjhaṅga—enlightenment factor (the 7)

***sambhava**—*also* being, existence, positive being: M I 261

***sambhava**—(encl.): implication (*tadattha-sambhava*: of that meaning, because that meaning is actually there): Khp-a 19, 106

sambhāra—accessory

sambhāveti—*also* to estimate, reckon, judge: Vism 321; Vism-a 313

***sambhuñjati**—to exploit, <to enjoy>: Dhs-a 110

***sambhoga**—*also* exploitation, <enjoyment>, making use of: Vism 461, 528

sammatta—rightness (the 8 and the 10)

sammatta-niyāma—certainty of rightness (term for 1st path)

sammā—right

sammā-diṭṭhi—right view {2 kinds: see M III 72; 5 kinds: M-a IV 135} [for def. see *diṭṭhi*)

sammā-samādhi—right concentration (5-factored: Vibh 334)

sammā-sambuddha—Fully Enlightened One (the 7)

sammukha—confrontation {4 kinds: M-a IV 43}

sammuti—convention, conventional: M-a I 25, 137-38

sammuti-dhamma—conventional idea: Vism-a 190

sammuti-sacca—conventional truth (e.g., *kasiṇa-paññatti*: It-a to It 44)

***sammussana**—forgetting

sammosa—forgetfulness

sammoha—delusion
sara—vowel (gram.)
saraṇa—refuge (the 3) [def. M-a I 130f.; Khp-a 13f.]
saraṇa—remembering
sa-raṇa—with conflict: M III 235; Dhs 1294
*__sarasandhi__—vowel-liaison (gram.)
*__sarūpena__—(adv.) in its own form: Vism 462, 508
sa-lakkhaṇa—specific characteristic (e.g., *kakkhalatā* of *paṭhavī*)
*__salākiya__—lancet, a lancet-user, remover of cataracts: Khp-a 21
salla—dart {5 kinds: Vibh 377; 7 kinds: Nidd I 59}
sallakkhaṇā—observation
sallakkheti—to observe
*__sallāna__—settling down: M-a I 181
*__sallekha__—effacement
saḷāyatana—the sixfold base [def. M I 52; III 215f., 258f.; S IV 1f.; Vibh 136; Vism 528, 562]
savana—hearing
savana—flowing
*__savana__—exudation: Vism 683 (cf. *pa-savana*)
*__saviggaha__—state of having an individual graspable entity: Vism-a 68
savyābajjhattabhāva—censurable personality {4 kinds: M-a IV 100}
*__sasaṅkhāra__—prompted: D III 237; Dhs 146
*__sasambhāra__—with its accessories (e.g., "empirical" *paṭhavī* as opposed to *paṭhavī-dhātu*): M-a I 25; Vism 445
*__sasambhāra-kathā__—accessory locution: Vism 20 (log.)
sassata—eternal
sassata-diṭṭhi—eternity view
sassata-vāda—theory of eternity (of the *attā*)
saha—with, together with

***sahakāra**—twin (2 fruits with 1 stalk): Khp-a 53
sahagata—accompanied by
sahajāta—conascent {7 kinds: Th-a II 221}
***sahaṭṭhāna**—co-present: Vism 432
***sahabyeti**—to accompany: Vism-a 371
sahabhū—co-existent with
***sahekaṭṭha**—*see*: *ekaṭṭha*
sahetuka—(consciousness) with root-cause (by being accompanied by *hetu*)
sā—(masc.) dog (*see*: *san* in PED)
***sākalla**—right, befitting: Khuddas 69
sāṭheyya—fraud
sāta—gratifying, gratification
***sātisaya**—(*sa* + *atisaya*) exceeding: Vism-a
sādhana—(1) accomplishing; (2) establishment of meaning of word (*see*: *kattu-*, *karaṇa-*, and *bhāva-*)
sādhāraṇa—common to, shared with
***sādhika**—accomplishing: Vism 146
***sāphalya**—fruitfulness: M-a I 167
***sāmaggī**—reconciliation, harmony
sāmañña—(1) general (adj.); (2) general usage (n.)
sāmañña—state of the monk, asceticism, (state of the *samaṇa*) [def. S V 25]
***sāmañña**—lover of *samaṇas*: D III 74
sāmañña-phala—fruits of asceticism
sāmañña-lakkhaṇa—general characteristics {the 3: anicca, *dukkha, anattā*}
sāmantajappā—indirect talk (Vibh 353; Vism-a 46)
***sāmivacana**—genitive case (gram.)
sāmukkaṃsika—peculiar to (*buddhānaṃ sāmukkaṃsika-desanā*: the teaching peculiar to Buddhas, i.e., the four noble truths): M I 380; A V 194; Vin I 16 (not as in PED)
sāra—core, heartwood {4 kinds: A II 141; Vism-a }

*__sāraṇa__—dispersal: Vism 612
*__sārambha__—presumption: M I 37; M-a I 170
sārammaṇa—that has an object
*__sārādheti__—to congratulate: Khp-a 231
*__sāli__—possessing, abounding in, full of: Dhs-a (name of Dhs-a = *Atthasālinī*)
sāvaka—disciple (hearer)
sāsana—message, instruction, dispensation
sāsava—affected by cankers
sikkhā—training
sikkhāpada—training precept
*__siṅga__—*also* foppery: Vibh 351
*__siṅgāra__—foppishness: Vibh 351
*__singhāṭaka__—*also* a tripod, and a road bifurcation: Khp-a 44, 206
*__siṭṭha__—prepared: Vism 491
siddhi—establishment (of word (*pada-*) or meaning (*attha-*) = *sādhana*, q.v.)
*__sineheti__—to liquefy: M-a I 268
sippa—craft {2 kinds: Vibh-a 410}
*__sippikā__—a bag: Vism 264
*__sippijā__—a kind of pearl: M-ṭ I 73
*__sibbanī__—the Seamstress (name of *taṇhā*): Sn 1042; A III 399-401; Dhs 1059
silā—stone, marble {8 kinds: M-ṭ I 74}
*__siliṭṭha__—consistent: M-a III 237
*__silesa__—cement: Vism 354
sīdanta—bottomless (name for ocean around Mt. Sineru): Vism-a 199
*__sīmā__—*also* boundary within which acts of Vinaya are carried out, "chapter-house": Vin I 106-107
sīla—virtue, custom, rite
*__sīlaka__—good-tempered: Vism 103

sīlana—composing: Vism 8

sīlabbata—(*sīla* + *vata*) virtue and duty, <rules and observances>

sīsa—head {2 kinds: S-a I 184; 13 kinds: Paṭis I 102}

sukkha-vipassaka—bare- (or dry-) insight worker

sukha—pleasure, pleasant [def. M I 302; Dhs 10; Vism 145, 461]

***sukha**—*also* tepid (of water): Vism 338

***sukhana**—act of pleasing: Vism 145

sukhallikānuyoga—devotion to pleasure {4 kinds: D III 130}

sukhuma-rūpa—subtle *rūpa* (i.e., all kinds except the 4 *mahā-bhūta*:) {16 kinds: Vism 450}

sugati—happy destination {3 *sugati-bhava*: Vism 650; Vism-a }

***suṅkaghātaka**—customs defrauder, tax evader: Khp-a 218

sucarita—good conduct {3 kinds: *kāya, vacī, mano*}

suñña, suññata—void

suññatā—voidness (*dvi-koṭikā, ti-koṭikā* and *catukoṭikā*): M-a IV 64; Vism 654; M-a II 112 {2 kinds: Comy. to Kv xix,2} [def. M III 104f., 109f.; Paṭis II 177f.]

***suṇhā**—daughter-in-law (*kula-suṇhā* = *suṇisā*): Vism 20

suta—heard [def. M-a I 4]

***sutavant**—well taught

***suttaka**—kind of worm in the body: Vism 258

***sudassana**—name of one of the 5 mountains surrounding Lake Anottatta: Vism 206; M-a III 35

suddhāvāsa—the Pure Abodes (the 5 heavens where the *anāgāmin* is reborn and attains nibbāna)

suddhika—bare: Dhs 343

***sunaka (sūnaka, suṇaka?)**—sausage? (*maṃsa-*): Khp-a 46

***sunibbuta**—quite extinguished: Vism 45

sunhāta— = *sunahāta* (Burmese spelling)

supina—a dream [def. Vibh-a 407; A-a III 316f.; Vin-a 520]

***subba**—ordinary (?) (*subba-tiṇāni*): M-a II 160
***subbata**—(*su* + *vata*) with good duties undertaken: Vism 45
subha—beauty, beautiful
***surati**—to shine: Ud-a 299
***surabhi**—perfume: Vism 100, 195, 339; Khp-a 129; Ja VI 236
***suvaca**—meek, amenable to verbal correction (not as in PED under *su*): Sn 143; M I 96
***suvaṇṇa**—a (gold) coin (5 s., or 25 s. = 1 *nikkha*: Vibh-mṭ 321)
***susukā**—*also* a shark (?): Vibh 376 (= *caṇḍa-maccha*: Vibh-a)
***sussuta**—well remembered
***suhajja**—companionship, companion: M III 266; A IV 96; Sn 37
***suhada**—companion: D III 187
***sūcayati**—to indicate, to betray (presence of): Vism 481
***sūci**—*also* kind of insect: M-a IV 156
***sūceti**—to hint: Vibh-a 475
sūdana—cleansing: Vism 372; M-a (name of M-a = Papañca-sūdanī)
***sūlī**—midwife (?): M-a IV 199 (?)
sekha—initate, <learner, one in training> {7 kinds: one who has attained any of the 4 paths and 1st 3 fruitions} [def. M-a I 40]
seṭṭha-bhāva—supremacy {3 kinds: Vibh-a }
senāsana—resting-place, lodging {the 9: see M I 181; 15 kinds: A-aA-a }
***semāna**—(p.pr. of *seti*) lying down: M I 88; III 179
seyya—mode of lying down {4 kinds: M-a II 316; A II 244}
sesa—remainder, rest (*katekasesa*: one member of group representing all or any of the others [log.]): Vism 561, 562; *ekasesanaya*: Vism-a 229; *see under*: *desa*
soka—sorrow [def. D II 305; Vism 503]
socana—act of sorrowing

soceyya—pureness {3 kinds: A I 271}

***soṇḍavant**—possessing a pond: Vism-a 116

sotāpatti—stream-entry (1st stage of realization)

sotāpanna—stream-enterer (one who has reached the 1st stage of realization)

sobhana—creditable, <beautiful>

somanassa—joy (6 *somanassopavicāra*: D III 244) [def. Dhs 18; Vism 461]

***svāvatthita**—well defined: Vibh 193

H

***haṃsa-vaṭṭaka**—<a decorative design having a circle of geese (?)> M-a II 268 (*haṃsa-vaṭṭakachannenā ti haṃsavaṭṭaka-paṭicchannena; haṃsa-maṇḍalākārenā ti attho*: Sp-ṭ)

***hattha**—*also* measure of length (from elbow to extended little-finger tip: 4 h. = 1 *yaṭṭhi;* 28 h. = 1 *abbhantara*)

***hatthagahita-pañha**—"hand-grasping question": Vism 266; Vibh-a 260

***hattha-pāsa**—hand's reach

***hatthikumbhajā**—kind of pearl: M-ṭ I 73

***hadati**—to defecate: Pv

hadaya—heart (either the physical organ or in the sense of "mind")

hadaya-vatthu—heart-basis (i.e., physical basis of *mano*)

***harampaccā**—(ger.) having brought back: Khuddas 21

***harita**—(pp. of *harati*) brought, carried

***haritaka**—gall-nut, myrobalan: Nidd I 225

***hassaka**—laughable, ridiculous: M II 201

***hāra**—necklace (*muttā-hāra* pearl-necklace): Vism 10

***hārakuta**—metal alloy: M-ṭ I 73

hiri—conscience, <shame> [def. Dhs 30; Vism 464]

hīna—(1) abandoned: M i.,38, 460; (2) inferior

***hīḷana**—self-loathing: Vibh-a 486

hetu—(1) reason, cause (loosely); (2) root-cause (technically: 3 *akusala*: Vibh 402; 3 *kusala*: Vibh 402; 3 *avyākata*: Vibh 402, 408 {4 kinds: Vibh-a 402; M-a IV 77; Paṭṭh 27; 6 kinds: Vibh 407; 8 kinds: Vibh 405} [def. Dhs-a 61]

honto—ppr. of *hoti*: Khp-a 239

PART II:

SUPPLEMENTARY GLOSSARIES

Grammatical Terms

Organized Listings

The 4 parts of speech (padajāti):

nāma—noun, substantive
ākhyāta—verb
upasagga—prefix
nipāta—particle
sandhi—liaison, euphonic junction:
sara-sandhi—vowel liaison
vyañjana-sandhi—vowel-consonant liaison
niggahīta-sandhi—liaison with *niggahīta*

Case-endings (vibhatti):

paccatta-vacana—nominative case (*paṭhamā*: first)
ālapana-vacana—vocative
upayoga-vacana—accusative (*dutiyā*: second)
karaṇa-vacana—instrumental (*tatiyā*: third)
sampadāna-vacana—dative (*catutthī*: fourth)
nissakka-vacana—ablative of separation (*pañcamī*: fifth)
itthambhūta-vacana—ablative of likeness
sāmi-vacana—genitive (*chaṭṭhī*: sixth)
bhumma-vacana—locative case (*sattamī*: seventh)

Words relating to substantives:

liṅga—gender (*liṅga-vipallāsa*: change of gender; *tīṇi liṅgāni*: 3 genders)
pulliṅga—masculine gender
itthiliṅga—feminine gender
napuṃsakaliṅga—neuter gender
ekavacana—singular
bahuvacana—plural
nāma-nāma—substantive, proper name

sabba-nāma—pronoun
guṇa-nāma—adjective
aniyamita—relative pronoun (e.g., *yaṃ*)
niyamita—demonstrative pronoun (e.g., *taṃ*)
samāsa-nāma—compound noun
taddhita-nāma—derivative from noun
kitaka-nāma—derivative from verb

The verb (ākhyāta):
kāla—tense
dhātu—verbal root (e.g., √*pā*)
rūpa—form of stem (e.g., *piva*)
vattamānakāla—present indicative tense
ajjatanī—aorist
bhavissantī—future indicative
pañcamī—imperative (mood)
sattamī—optative (mood)
hīyattanī—imperfect
parokkhā—perfect
kālātipatti—conditional
kārita—causative
tumanta—infinitive
parassapada—active
attanopada—middle (reflexive)
kammapada—passive
kāraka—voice
kattukāraka—active voice
kammakāraka—passive voice
bhūvādigaṇa—first conjugation (e.g., √*bhū*)
rudhādigaṇa—second conjugation (e.g., √*rudh*)
divādigaṇa—third conjugation (e.g., √*div*)
suvādigaṇa—fourth conjugation (e.g., √*su*)
kiyādigaṇa—fifth conjugation (e.g., √*ki*)

tanādigaṇa—sixth conjugation (e.g., √*tan*)
curādigaṇa—seventh conjugation (e.g., √*cur*)
purisa—person
paṭhama-purisa—third person (N.B.)
majjhima-purisa—second person
uttama-purisa—first person
akammaka—intransitive
sakammaka—transitive
dvikammaka—bitransitive

The particle (nipāta):
paṭisedha—negative (*na, no, mā*)
sampiṇḍana—conjunction (*ca, pi*)
kriyā, kiriya—adverb, predicate
samuccaya—conjunction (*ca*)
saṃyoga—conjunction (*ca*)

The prefix (upasagga):
ati, adhi, anu, apa, api, abhi, ava (= o), ā, u, upa, du, ni, nī, pa, pati, parā, pari, vi, saṃ, su

Compounds (samāsa):
(1) **kammadhāraya**—adjectival compound [adj. + subs.] (e.g., *niluppalaṃ*: the blue waterlily)
(2) **digu**—numerical determinative compound [num. + subs.]
(a) **samāhāra**—collective grammatically singular termination (e.g., *tilokaṃ*: the three worlds)
(b) **asamāhāra**—individual plural termination (e.g., *pañcindriyāni*: the five faculties)
(3) **tappurisa**—dependent determinative compound [subs. in oblique case + subs. or adj.]
(a) **dutiyā-tappurisa** [acc. subs. + subs. or adj.] (e.g., *gāmagato* = *gāmaṃ gato*: gone to the village)

(b) tatiyā-tappurisa [instr. subs. + subs. or adj.] (e.g., *buddhadesito = buddhena desito*: taught by the Buddha)

(c) catutthī-tappurisa [dat. subs. + subs. or adj.] (e.g., *pāsādadabbaṃ = pāsādāya dabbaṃ*: material for the palace)

(d) pañcamī-tappurisa [abl. of sep. subs. + subs. or adj.] (e.g., *rukkhapatito = rukkhā patito*: fallen from the tree)

(e) chaṭṭhī-tappurisa [gen. subs. + subs. or adj.] (e.g., *jinavacanaṃ = jinassa vacanaṃ*: the word of the Conqueror)

(f) sattamī-tappurisa [loc. subs + subs. or adj.] (e.g., *gāmavāsī = gāme vāsī*: dweller in a village)

alutta-samāsa [inflected subs. + subs. or adj.] (e.g., *manasikāro = manasi kāro*: keeping in mind, attention)

upapada-tappurisa—verbal dependent determinative compound [subs. + verbal subs.] (e.g., *kumbhakāro = kumbhaṃ kāro*: pot-maker, potter)

(4) dvanda—copulative compound [subs. + subs.]

(a) samāhāra: with singular termination (e.g., *hatthassarathapattikaṃ = hatthino ca assā ca rathā ca pattikā ca*: elephants, horses, chariots, and infantry)

(b) asamāhāra: with plural termination (e.g., *candasuriyā = cando ca suriyo ca*: the moon and the sun)

(5) avyayībhāva—adverbial compound [indecl. adv. + subs.] (e.g., *upanagaraṃ = upa + nagaraṃ*: near the town)

(6) bahubbīhi—relative compound [combination of subs, + subs. used as adj. to qualify another subs.] (e.g., *lohitamakkhitasīso (puriso) = (purisassa) lohitena makkhitaṃ sīsaṃ (atthi)*: (a man) whose head is smeared with blood)

missaka-samāsa—complex compound (e.g., *suranaramahito = (a) surā ca narā ca* (dvanda); (b) *suranarehi mahito* (tappurisa): honoured by gods and men)

Secondary derivatives (taddhita) [subs. (or subs. + suffix) + suffix]:

(1) sāmañña-taddhita—general secondary derivative

(a) **appaccattha**—denoting lineage (suffixes = *(ṇ)a, (ṇ)āna, (ṇ)era, (ṇ)eyya*)
(b) **anekattha**—of various meanings (suffixes = *(ṇ)ika, (ṇ)a, ima, iya, tā, ka, maya*)
(c) **atthyattha**—denoting endowment, possession (suffixes = *ava, ala, ila, ika, ī, vī, ssī, vantu, mantu*)
(d) **saṅkhyā**—numerical derivatives [number + suffix] (suffixes = *ma, tiya, ttha, ī, ka*)

(2) **bhāva-taddhita**—gerundial used as abstract subs. [subs. + suffix] (suffixes = *tā, tta, ttana, (ṇ)ya, (ṇ)a*)
(3) **avyaya-taddhita**—indeclinable numbers and adverbs (e.g., num. + *kkhattum* (adv.), *dhā, so, thā, tana*)

Primary derivative (kitaka)[verbal root + suffix = substantive]:

(1) **kicca**—for formation of passive participles (suffixes = *tabba, anīya, (ṇ)ya, (ṇ)iya, tayya, icca*)
(2) **kita**—for formation of active participles or nouns expressing an active meaning (suffixes = *nta, māna, ta,* etc.)

Establishment of word-meaning (pada-siddhi, sadda-siddhi)

(1) **karaṇa-sādhana**—definition by way of instrumental sense (e.g., *saranti etāyā ti sati*: by this they are mindful, thus it is mindfulness)
(2) **kattu-sādhana**—definition by way of agent (e.g., *sayaṃ saratī ti sati:* this itself is mindful, thus it is mindfulness)
(3) **bhāva-sādhana**—definition by way of state (e.g., *saraṇamattam eva esā ti sati*: this is mere being mindful, thus it is mindfulness)

Vocabulary

akammaka—intransitive verb
akkhara—letter (of alphabet)
accantasaṃyoga—direct governance (of acc. by transitive verb)
ajjatanī—aorist (tense)

atidesa—extension of meaning
atītakāla—past tense
attanopada—middle (voice)
adhikaraṇa—one kind of locative (= container)
anāgatakāla—future tense
aniyamita—relative pronoun
aniyamuddesa—relative clause
anunāsika—the letter *ṃ*, the nasal
anussāra—the letter *ṃ*, the nasal
anekattha—type of suffix
apādāna—function of ablative, i.e., separation
appaccattha—type of suffix
alutta—type of compound (see above)
avayava—constituent of compound
avuddhika—weak strengthening of root in vowel gradation
avyaya—indeclinable
avyaya-taddhita—indeclinable numerals and adverbs
avyayībhāva—adverbial compound
asamāhāra—(compound) with plural termination
ākhyāta—verb
ādhāra—locative, support
ālapana—vocative case
itaritara—dvanda with plural ending
itthambhūta-vacana—ablative of likeness
itthiliṅga—feminine gender
uttama-purisa—first person
upacāra—figure of speech, metaphor
upapada-tappurisa—verbal dependent determinative compound
upayoga-vacana—accusative case
upasa—prefixed vowel
upasagga—prefix, suffix, affix

ekavacana—singular
okāsa—locative case
kattā—subject of verb
kattukāraka—active voice
kattusādhana—definition of word by way of agent
kamma—object of word
kammakāraka—passive voice
kammadhāraya—adjectival compound
karaṇa-vacana—instrumental case
karaṇa-sādhana—definition of word by way of instrumental sense
kāra—letter or syllable (e.g., *makāro* = the letter *ma*)
kāraka—voice (of verb); syntax
kārita—causative
kāla—tense
kālātipatti—conditional derivative substantive
kicca—function, kind of verbal noun suffix
kita—verbal noun suffix
kitaka—verbal noun suffix
kiriyavisesa—adverb
kriyā, kiriya—adverb, predicate of verb
gaṇa—conjugation
guṇa—strong vowel gradation
guṇa-nāma—quality noun, adjective
catutthī—dative case
chaṭṭhī—genitive case
tatiya—instrumental case
taddhita—secondary derivative substantive
tappurisa—dependent determinative compound
tumanta—infinitive
tumicchattha—desiderative
digu—numerical determinative compound

dutiya—accusative case
dvanda—copulative compound
dvikammaka—bitransitive verb
dhātu—verbal root or stem
dhāturūpakasadda—denominative
napuṃsakaliṅga—neuter gender
nāma—noun, substantive
nāmā-nāma—noun
niggahīta—the final letter *ṃ*
nipāta—particle
nibbacana—derivative form, derivation
niyamita—demonstrative pronoun (e.g., *taṃ*)
nissaka-vacana—ablative of separation
nissita-vacana—dependent locution (cf. Vism 20, Vism-a 40)
paccatta-vacana—nominative case
paccaya—suffix
paccuppanna (kāla)—present (time)
pañcamī—imperative (mood); ablative of separation (case)
paṭisedha—negative (*na, no, mā*)
paṭhamā—nominative case
pada—word; syllable; phrase; sentence
padaccheda—contraction, elision of word
padalopa—elision of a word
pada-siddhi—establishment of word-meaning
parassapada—active (voice)
pariyāya—metaphor
parokkhā—perfect tense
puthuvacana—plural
pubbakiriya—gerund
purisa—person
pulliṅga—masculine gender
bahubbīhi—relative compound

bahuvacana—plural
bhavissantī—future (tense)
bhāva—state; a kind of verbal noun; abstract noun
bhāva-taddhita—gerundial
bhāva-napuṃsaka—neuter desiderative abstract noun
bhāva-sādhana—definition of word by way of state
bhāvena bhāvalakkhaṇa-bhummaṃ—locative absolute
bhumma-vacana—locative case
majjhima-purisa—second person
missaka-samāsa—mixed compound
missakiriya—present participle
rūpa—form of stem or root
lakāra—tense (of verb)
liṅga—gender; word stem
vaṇṇa—phonetically distinct sound
vattamānakāla—present tense
vākya—sentence
vikappa-samāhāra—dvanda with either sing. or plural ending
vibhatti—case ending
vibhatti-lopa—elision of case ending
viyoga—disjunction (*vā*)
visesana—"distinguishing," i.e., adjective
visesana-parapada—*kammadhāraya* (second member qualifying first)
visesana-pubbapada—*kammadhāraya* (first member qualifying second)
vuddhi—lengthened vowel gradation
vyañjana—consonant
vyatireka—negative
saṃyoga—conjunction (e.g., *ca, pi*)
sakammaka—transitive verb

saṅkhā—number (in word formation)
saṅkhya-taddhita—numerical derivative
sattamī—optative (mood); locative (case)
sadda—word
sadda-sattha—grammar
sadda-siddhi—establishment of word-meaning
sandhi—liaison
sabba-nāma—pronoun
samāsa—compound noun
samāhāra—compound with singular termination
samuccaya—conjunction (e.g., *ca, pi*)
sampadāna-vacana—dative case
sampiṇḍana—conjunction, abbreviation
sambandha—construction
sara—vowel
sasambhārakathā—substitutional location (cf. Vism 20, Vism-a 40)
sādhana-siddhi—derivation of word
sāmañña—general
sāmi-vacana—genitive case
hīyattanī—imperfect (tense)

Plants & Flowers

akka—(Sinh. *varā*): Vism 249
***ariṭṭhaka**—kind of creeper (Sinh. *penela*): Vism 249
alābu, lābu—pumpkin (Sinh. *labu*): Vism 251
assattha—pippul, Bo tree (Sinh. *äsatu*): D II 4; Vism 183
ākulī—kind of flower (Sinh. *raṇavarā*): Vism 260
uppala—water lily (Sinh. *upul*): D I 75; M I 169 (= S I 138)
eraṇḍa, elaṇḍa—castor-oil plant: M II 152
kacchaka—kind of tree (Sinh. *kalusuya*): Vism 183
kaṇavīra—oleander (Sinh. *kaṇeru*): Vism 183
kaṇikāra—tree with yellow flowers (Sinh. *kinihirimal*): D II 111; Vism 173
kataka—kind of seed, "clearing nut" (Sinh. *ingini*): Vism 254
kandaḷa—kind of yam (Sinh. *kandala*): D I 264; Vism 253, 254, 255
kapiṭṭhaka, kapitthana—wood-apple (Sinh. *divul*): Vism 183
kamala—lotus (Sinh. *piyum*): Vism 250
karañja—a tree used medicinally (Sinh. *karanda* or *magul karanda*): Khp-a 46
karamaṇḍa—kind of bush (Sinh. *kaḷu*): Vism 183
kālavalli—black creeper (Sinh. *kaḷu*): Vism 183
kiṃsuka—tree with red flowers (Sinh. *käla*): Vism 196, 252
kumuda—white water-lily (Sinh. *kumudu, hälmäli*): Vism 174, 256
kuvalaya—blue water-lily (Sinh. *mahanil*): Vism 250
kumbaṇḍī—sweet melon (Sinh. *komaḍu*): Vism 183
***ketakī**—screw-pine (Sinh. *vätakeyya*): Khp-a 46
koraṇḍaka—red flower (Sinh. *karaṇḍu*): Vism 174, 183
koviḷāra—kind of tree with red flowers (Sinh. *koppila*): A IV 117; Sn 44; Vism 257
kosātaki—loofah gourd (Sinh. *väṭakolu*): Vism 256, 260
khajjūrika—wild date palm: Khp-a 49

girikaṇṇikā—blue morning glory (Sinh. *nil kaṭaroḷu*): Vism 173
candana—sandalwood (Sinh. *sandun*): M II 152
jayasumana—red flower: Vism 174
tagara—shrub yielding a fragrant powder: It 68; Khp-a 128
tāla—palmyra palm: Vism 250
tumba—calabash gourd: Khp-a 44
dakasītalika—white water-lily (Sinh. *hälmäli*): Vism 258
dambuli—pomegranate
nāgabalā—leaf with white juice (Sinh. *käliyakola*): Vism 261
nālikera—coconut palm (Sinh. *polgaha*)
nigguṇḍi—blue flower (Sinh. *nika*): Vism 257
nigrodha—banyan (Sinh. *nuga*): Vism 183
niluppala—blue lotus (Sinh. *nilupul*): Vism 173
pattaṅga—yellow flower (Sinh. *patangi mal*): Vism 173
paduma—white lotus (Sinh. *häl piyum, nelum*): Vism 174; D I 75; M I 169 (= S I 138)
padumaka—kind of scented wood: M II 152
pāḷibaddhaka—red flower (Sinh. *erabadu*): Vism 256; Khp-a 46
puṇḍarīka—white lotus: D I 75; M I 169 (= S I 138)
punnāga—kind of tree bearing fruit (Sinh. *domba*): Vism 254, 256; Khp-a 50
pūtilatā—stinking creeper (Sinh. *rasakinda*): Vism 183; Khp-a 47
bandhujīvaka—hibiscus flower (Sinh. *bandu*): D II 111; Vism 174
makaci—kind of fibre (Sinh. *niyanda*): Vism 249
maṇila—kind of tree: Vism 313
mallikā—jasmine (Sinh. *däsaman*): Vism 251
lābu (= alābu)—pumpkin (Sinh. *labu*): Vism 183
lodda—leaf used for washing robes (Sinh. *bombu*): Vin-vn
vassikā—jasmine (Sinh. *däsaman*): Vism 174

veḷu—bamboo (Sinh. *uṇa*): Vism 1

salaḷa—kind of scented wood: M II 152

sāla—kind of scented wood: M II 152

sāmā—brown creeper (Sinh. *pūḍā*): Vism 183

sinduvāra, sindhavāra—kind of flower (Sinh. *nika*): Vism 105

sumana—(Arabian) jasmine (Sinh. *däsaman*): Vism 174, 250

hata—mushroom (?) (Sinh. *hatu*): A II 206

haliddā—turmeric (Sinh. *kaha*): Vism 250

Months & Seasons

(Source: Vis 621 and Ṭīkā)

Season	Sub-season	Month	Equivalent
hemanta (cold)	*hemanta* (winter)	*māgasira* *phussa*	Nov-Dec Dec-Jan
	sisira (cool)	*māgha* *phagguna*	Jan-Feb Feb-Mar
gimhāna (heat)	*vasanta* (spring)	*citta* *vesākha*	Mar-Apr Apr-May
	gimha (summer)	*jeṭṭha* *āsāḷha*	May-Jun Jun-July
vassāna (rains)	*vassāna* (rains)	*sāvana* *poṭṭhapāda*	July-Aug Aug-Sep
	sārada (autumn)	*assayuja* *kattika*	Sep-Oct Oct-Nov

Note: The Indian month begins on the first day of the waning moon and ends on the full moon.

Numbers & Measures

High numbers (Nett-a 220)

koṭi = 10,000,000
pakoṭi = 100 x 100,000 *koṭi*
koṭippakoṭi = 100 x 100,000 *pakoṭi*
nahuta = 100 x 100,000 *koṭippakoṭi*
ninnahuta = 100 x 100,000 *nahuta*
abbuda = 100 x 100,000 *ninnahuta*
nirabbuda = 20 *abbuda*
aṭaṭa = 20 *nirabbuda*
ahaha = 20 *aṭaṭa*
kumuda = 20 *ahaha*
sogandhika = 20 *kumuda*
uppala = 20 *sogandhika*
puṇḍarīka = 20 *uppala*
paduma = 20 *puṇḍarīka*

High numbers (Nett-a 259, Abh v. 475f.)

koṭi = a unit of 7 ciphers (10,000,000)
pakoṭi = a unit of 14 ciphers
koṭippakoṭi = a unit of 21 ciphers
nahuta = a unit of 28 ciphers
ninnahuta = a unit of 35 ciphers
akkhobhaṇī = a unit of 42 ciphers
bindhu = a unit of 49 ciphers
abbuda = a unit of 56 ciphers
nirabbuda = a unit of 63 ciphers
ahaha = a unit of 70 ciphers
ababa = a unit of 77 ciphers
aṭaṭa = a unit of 84 ciphers
sogandhika = a unit of 91 ciphers

uppala = a unit of 98 ciphers
kumuda = a unit of 105 ciphers
puṇḍarīka = a unit of 112 ciphers
paduma = a unit of 119 ciphers
kathāna = a unit of 126 ciphers
mahākathāna = a unit of 133 ciphers
asaṅkheyya = a unit of 140 ciphers

Measures of capacity (Nett-a 219)
kosala pattha = 4 *māgadhaka pattha*
āḷhaka = 4 *kosala pattha*
doṇa = 4 *āḷhaka*
māṇikā = 4 *doṇa*
khāri = 4 *māṇikā*
vāha = 20 *khāri*
sakaṭa = *vāha*

Measures of capacity (Vinayālaṅkāra I p.102 Be, Sp-ṭ II p. 427 Be, Abh)
kuṭuva (kuḍuba) = 4 *muṭṭhi*
pattha (patta) = 4 *kuṭuva*
nāli = *pattha*
āḷhaka = *tumba*
doṇa = 4 *āḷhaka* (or 4 *tumba*)
māṇikā = 4 *doṇa*
khāri = 4 *māṇikā*
vāha = 20 *khāri*
sakaṭa = *vāha* (Nett-a 219, Sn-a 476)
vāha = 2 *sakaṭa* (M-a III 287)

Units of length (Vibh-a 343, Abh v. 196-97)
paramāṇu = "atom"
aṇu = 36 *paramāṇu*
tajjārī = 36 *aṇu*

rathareṇu = 36 *tajjārī*
likkhā = 36 *rathareṇu*
ūkā = 7 *likkhā*
dhaññamāsa—rice grain = 7 *ūkā*
aṅgula—finger = 7 *dhaññamāsa*
vidatthi—span = 12 *aṅgula*
ratana—cubit = 2 *vidatthi*
yaṭṭhi—pole = 7 *ratana*
usabha = 20 *yaṭṭhi*
gāvuta = 80 *usabha*
yojana—league = 4 *gāvuta*

Units of length:
hattha—hand = elbow to fingertip
muṭṭhi—fist = elbow to knuckles (?)
vidatthi—span = thumb to little finger extended
byāma—fathom = head to foot
porisa—man's height = foot to fingertips of upheld arm
sugatavidatthi—"Buddha span" = 3 *vidatthi*
yuga = 9 *vidatthi*
yaṭṭhi—pole = 4 *hattha*
abbhantara = 28 *hattha*
usabha = 20 *yaṭṭhi*

Money
pāda = 5 (or 2) *māsaka*
kahāpana = 4 *pāda*
nikkha = 5 *suvaṇṇa* (M-a IV 151)
nikkha = 20 or 25 *suvaṇṇa* (M-ṭ to above)

Sanskrit Logical Terms

(See S. Kuppuswami Sastri, *Primer of Indian Logic*)

Four conditions for knowledge

pramātṝ—subject, knower
prameya—object, the known
pramiti—state of knowledge
pramāṇa—means or category of knowing

Four means of knowing (pramāṇa)

pratyakṣa—direct perception, personal experience
anumāna—inference
upamāna—comparison, analogy
sabda—verbal testimony

The syllogism of five terms (nyāya-vaiśeṣika system) (see Vism-a 581-82; Kathāvatthu trans., p. 1)

(a) pratijñā (paṭiññā)—proposition

[The mountain (*pakṣa, pakkha* = subject) has fire (*sādhya* = probandum).]

(b) hetu—reason

[For it has smoke (*liṅga* = probans).] (Note: Strictly, *pakṣa* = the mountain having smoke.)

(c) udāharaṇa—example

[Whatever has smoke (*liṅgaparāmāsa* = subsumption of probans) has fire (*vyāpti, vyatti* = concomitance of *sādhya* and *liṅga*), like a hearth (*udāharaṇa* = example).]

(d) upanaya, upanayana—deduction, application

[And so is this.]

(e) nigamana—conclusion

[Therefore it is such.]—This may be shortened to three members

(a), (b), (c), or (c), (d), (e), and (c) may even be omitted leaving only (d) and (e).

VOCABULARY

ativyāpti—definition with too wide a scope
anavasthā—infinite regress
anityadoṣa—occasional defect
anupasaṃhārin—non-conclusive
anubhūti—perception
anumāna—inference
anumiti—inference
anusandhāna—(= *upanaya*)
anaikanta, anaikantika—over-generalized, inconclusive (= *savyabhicāra*)
anvaya—affirmation, positive
apadeśa—(= *hetu*)
apekṣa—relative
aprayojakatvaśaṅkā—doubt about an exception
abādhitatva—not being invalidated by a stronger proof
abhāva—non-existence
abhidheyatva—nameableness
artha—sense object
arthāpatti—presumptive conclusion
avacchedaka—invariable
avayava—part of whole
avayavin—composite whole
avinābhāva—non-existence in the absence of (= *pūrvapakṣavyāpti*)
avyāpti—definition with too narrow a scope
asatpratipakṣitatva—non-vitiation by a counter-probans
asambhava—inappropriate definition
asiddha—unestablished
asiddhi—non-establishment
āgama—verbal testimony

āśrayāsiddha—unestablished with respect to abode, e.g., "sky-flowers"
indriya—sense faculty
uttara—response
utpatti—production
udāharaṇa—example
upanaya—deduction, application
upamāna—analogy
upādhi—adventitious factor
karaṇa—instrument
kṝtakava—produceability
kevalānvayin—inconceivable
guṇa—quality
cakraka—circular argument
chala—quibbling
jalpa—successful advocacy, wrangling
jāti—genus
jāti—futile replies or objections
tattvādhyavasāya—establishment of truth
tadātmya—identity
tadutpatti—causality
tarka—reasoning, indirect argument or proof
duṣṭahetu—(= *hetvābhāsa*)
dṝṣṭānta—example
doṣa—defect, flaw (in reasoning)
dharmin—thing qualified, minor term
nigamana—conclusion
nigrahasthāna—weakness; occasion for reproof
nityadoṣa—permanent defect
nidarśana—(= *udāharaṇa*)
nirṇaya—determination of the truth
nyāya—general rule, axiom; logical or syllogistic argument

nyāyaprayoga—syllogism
pakṣa—subject; a thesis, proposition to be proved
pakṣadharmatā—presence of reason (*hetu*) in subject (*pakṣa*)
parāmāsa—subsumption
pūrvapakṣalakṣaṇa—provisional character of the proof
pūrvapakṣavyāpti—provisional concomitance of the proof
pratijñā—proposition
pratiyogin—counter-correlative
pratyakṣa—direct perception, personal experience
pratyabhijñā—recognition of a thing seen before
pramayatva—knowability
pramāṇa—means or category of knowing
prameya—object of knowledge
bādhita—overruled by a more cogent proof, i.e., by sensory experience
buddhi—sensory knowledge, sensation
bhinna—differentiated
bhūyodarśana—repeated observation
yukti—logic
lakṣana—characteristic, attribute; definition
lāghava—economy, parsimony
liṅga—reason, mark, probans
vāda—discussion; doctrine, proposition
vitaṇḍa—cavil, destructive criticism
vipakṣa—counter-example
viruddha—self-contradictory
vyatireka—negation
vyabhicāra—exception, irregularity
vyāpaka—concomitant, the pervading
vyāpāra—intermediate cause
vyāpti—concomitance, pervasion
vyāpya—the pervaded

vyāpyatvāsiddha—unestablished with respect to concomitance

śabda—verbal testimony

saṃśaya—doubt

sattā—existence

satpratipakṣa—vitiated by having an opposite

saṃdigdha—dubious reason

saṃnikarṣa—contact of senses with their objects

sapakṣa—similar instance

samavāya—inherence, inseparable concomitance

samprayoga—presentation of a part or aspect instead of the whole

savyabhicāra—inconclusive argument; vitiated by exception, not invariable

sādhana—demonstration, proof; reason (middle term) in proof

sādhya—thesis to be proved (major term, probandum)

sādhāraṇa—common, shared

sāhacaryaniyama—constant co-existence

siddha—established

siddhāntalakṣaṇa—characteristic of a completely established truth

siddhāntavyāpti—concomitance with a completely established truth

siddhi—establishment

svarūpa—own form

svarūpāsiddha—unestablished with respect to its own form, e.g., "sound is visible"

hetu—reason, middle term

hetudoṣa—defect in a reason

hetvābhāsa—fallacy; apparent but false reason

About the Author

Osbert Moore (as the author was known in lay life) was born on the 25th June 1905, in England. He graduated at Exeter College, Oxford, and during the Second World War he served as an army staff-officer in Italy. It was at that time, by reading an Italian book on Buddhism, that his interest in that teaching was aroused. This book—*The Doctrine of Awakening* by J. Evola—was later translated by a friend and fellow-officer, Harold Musson, who, in 1948, accompanied Osbert Moore to Ceylon. In 1949, both received novice ordination as Buddhist monks, at the Island Hermitage, Dodanduwa; and in 1950, the higher ordination as bhikkhus, via the Vajirarama Monastery, Colombo. Osbert Moore, our author, received the monastic name of Ñāṇamoli, and his friend that of Ñāṇavīra. Both returned soon to the Island Hermitage (an island monastery situated in a lagoon) where the Venerable Ñāṇamoli spent almost his entire monk life of eleven years. Only very rarely did he leave the quietude of the island, and it was on one of these rare occasions, on a walking tour undertaken with the senior monk of the Hermitage, that he suddenly passed away on 8th March 1960, through heart failure. He had not yet completed his 55th year. His death took place at a lonely little village, Veheragama near Maho.

In addition to the present volume, he translated, from the original Pali into lucid English, some of the most difficult texts of Theravāda Buddhism. These translations, listed below, were remarkable achievements in quantity as well as in quality. His translations show the highest standard of careful and critical scholarship and a keen and subtle mind philosophically trained. His work in this field is a lasting contribution to Buddhist studies.

Bhikkhu Ñāṇamoli: A Bibliography

Published by the Buddhist Publication Society

The Path of Purification (*Visuddhimagga*) by Bhadantācariya Buddhaghosa. Trans. 1956. 5th ed. 1991.

The Practice of Loving-kindness. Texts compiled and translated from the Pali. (Wheel No. 7) 1958.

Three Cardinal Discourses of the Buddha. Trans. with introduction and notes. (Wheel No. 17) 1960.

Pathways of Buddhist Thought. Essays. (Wheel No. 52/53) 1963.

Mindfulness of Breathing (*Ānāpānasati*). Texts compiled and translated from the Pali. 1964.

A Thinker's Notebook. Posthumous papers. 1972.

The Life of the Buddha according to the Pali Canon. 1972. 4th ed. 2006.

Published by the Pali Text Society

Minor Readings and The Illustrator. Trans. of Khuddakapāṭha and Commentary. 1960.

The Guide. Trans. of *Nettippakaraṇa*. 1962.

The Piṭaka Disclosure. Trans. of *Peṭakopadesa*. 1964.

The Path of Discrimination. Trans. of Paṭisambhidāmagga. 1982.

The Dispeller of Delusion. Trans. of *Sammohavinodanī*. 2 vols. 1987, 1991.

Published by Wisdom Publications

The Middle Length Discourses of the Buddha. Trans. of Majjhima Nikāya.

Of related interest from BPS

THE PATH OF PURIFICATION
The Visuddhimagga
Translated from the Pali by Bhikkhu Ñāṇamoli

The Visuddhimagga is the "great treatise" of Theravāda Buddhism, an encyclopedic manual of Buddhist doctrine and meditation written in the 5th century by the Buddhist commentator Bhadantācariya Buddhaghosa. The author's intention in composing this book is to organize the various teachings of the Buddha, found throughout the Pali Canon, into a clear and comprehensive path leading to the final Buddhist goal, Nibbāna, the state of complete purification. In the course of his treatise Buddhaghosa gives full and detailed instructions on the forty subjects of meditation aimed at concentration; an elaborate account of the Buddhist Abhidhamma philosophy; and detailed descriptions of the stages of insight culminating in final liberation. The translation by Bhikkhu Ñāṇamoli ranks as an outstanding cultural achievement.

BP 207H Hardback, 950 pp.

AN ANALYSIS OF THE PALI CANON
Edited by Russell Webb

A full analysis of the scriptures of Theravada Buddhism, with brief resumes of the principal suttas, a bibliography of translations from the Canon, grammars, and a section on Pali commentarial literature.

BP 607S Softback, 112 pp.

Of related interest from BPS

BUDDHIST DICTIONARY
Manual of Buddhist Terms and Doctrines
Ñāṇatiloka Thera

Since its first publication in 1952, Buddhist Dictionary has been a trusted companion and helper in the study of Buddhist literature. The author, the well-known German scholar-monk Ñāṇatiloka Thera (1879-1957), was qualified as few others have ever been to serve as a reliable guide through the field of Buddhist terminology and doctrine. This book offers authentic and lucid explanations of Buddhist Pali terms, with cross references in English and source references as well. Amidst the welter of modern books on Buddhism, and translations differing one from the other, this book will help in identifying the doctrinal terms and in correcting misleading renderings. Not a mere word dictionary but an aid to the terminology of Theravada Buddhism, Buddhist Dictionary will be as helpful to the serious lay student as to the professional scholar.

BP 601S Softback, 265 pp.

THE PALI LITERATURE OF CEYLON
G.P. Malalasekera

An old classic by the doyen of Sri Lanka's Pali scholars; admirably surveys Sri Lanka's rich legacy of Pali Buddhist literature. The book is also a gracefully written history of Sri Lankan Buddhism.

BP 610S Softback, 350 pp.

THE BUDDHIST PUBLICATION SOCIETY

The BPS is an approved charity dedicated to making known the Teaching of the Buddha, which has a vital message for people of all creeds. Founded in 1958, the BPS has published a wide variety of books and booklets covering a great range of topics. Its publications include accurate annotated translations of the Buddha's discourses, standard reference works, as well as original contemporary expositions of Buddhist thought and practice. These works present Buddhism as it truly is—a dynamic force which has influenced receptive minds for the past 2500 years and is still as relevant today as it was when it first arose.

For more information about the BPS and our publications please visit our website at http://www.bps.lk or send an e-mail to bps@sltnet.lk, or write a letter to:

The Administrative Secretary
BUDDHIST PUBLICATION SOCIETY

P.O. Box 61
54, Sangharaja Mawatha Kandy o Sri Lanka
E-mail: bps@sltnet.lk
Web site: http://www.bps.lk
Tel: +94 81 2237283
Fax: +94 81 2223679